GW00672070

# Leeds: a history of its tramways

NOEL PROUDLOCK

ISBN 0 9517185 0 9



Published by J. N. D. Proudlock
181 West Park Drive (West)
Leeds LS8 2BE

Typeset by Scarborough Typesetting Services and printed in Great Britain by MacDonald Lindsay Pindar, Edinburgh

A CIP catalogue record for this book is available from the British Library

Frontispiece Where it all began. The junction of the Moortown and Roundhay routes at Sheepscar. English Electric Chamberlain No 78 negotiates relaying work when the junction was re-aligned – note double overhead, 27 Apl 1951 (author)

# Contents

TETLEY'S
VICTORIA
1
LAWNSWOOD
Always ask for
Yorkshire Relish
TRUSTEE SAVINGS BANK
KEEP
LEFT

# Preface

29 October 1891 was a day of major significance both for Leeds and for the development of electricity as a power source for public transport when on that day the first vehicles in Europe to receive current through a roof mounted collector from an overhead supply wire operated from Sheepscar to Oakwood, at that time the entrance to Roundhay Park. Full public service started on 10 November 1891 and was continued successfully until 31 July 1896. This book is published as my personal commemoration of the centenary of that event, a hundred years during which developments have reached a point beyond the wildest imagination of those present on the day.

Leeds was a fast growing town with a great civic pride at the time the tramcar began to spread over Great Britain. No civic decisions of that time had a more profound effect on the city than the introduction of horse drawn trams by the Leeds Tramways Company in 1871, the subsequent purchase of the system by the Corporation in 1894 (the year after incorporation as a city) and its electrification from 1897 to 1902. As well as the very important event already referred to Leeds also scored firsts with the Maley combined electro-magnetic and mechanical track brake in 1907 and with trackless trams (trolley buses) in 1911. The city was also very early in the field with motor buses (1906), reserved tracks (1922), roller bearings and air brakes (1926) and modern high speed cars (1933).

I have therefore attempted to produce a compact history of the city's street rail transport, not ignoring the growth of the buses which ultimately replaced the trams in 1959, and to relate it to the general history of the city, especially to housing development on which the early electric tram system had a profound effect.

A very different picture is to be seen in many European cities where the principles recommended for Leeds in 1944–50 were adopted and very modern rail systems have developed. There is now increasing interest in similar new developments in America and Great Britain and it seems a pity that Leeds missed the opportunity to repeat its great pioneering role of 1897–1906.

In piecing together during 1968 that part of the story up to 1940 which I did not witness personally I have examined the Annual Reports of the Tramways and later Transport Committee to the Leeds City Council and various other volumes in the Local History Section of Leeds Public Library and must acknowledge the help of the staff in that section at the time in bringing out and putting away so many heavy volumes. I must also particularly acknowledge the assistance afforded at the same period by Mr. J. R. Blakeborough in allowing me to examine the tramcar records retained by Leeds City Transport as well as the photographs and negatives in their possession. Prints of some of these and also some from the *Yorkshire Post* and Leeds City Library collections are included and I acknowledge their courtesy in giving permission for their reproduction.

*Leeds February 1991* — *Noel Proudlock*

**Plate 1** One of the first type of car built by Leeds Corporation in 1908/9, No. 120 in original condition about 1911

*(Copyright Yorkshire Post Newspapers)*

CHAPTER 1

# Early public transport – the start of the tramway era

Provision of a regular service of vehicles for movement of people about an urban area is historically a relatively recent innovation and in Leeds among the first such services of which record remains was a local stage coach operated by Isaac Morley between the Cardigan Arms at Bramley and the Griffin Hotel in the town. A copy of the poster has for many years been exhibited in the street in the Abbey House Museum at Kirkstall advertising it to run four times each way on Tuesdays and Saturdays and once on other days 'for the convenience of cloth merchants on Market days'. Morley also advertised aims still very appropriate to public transport operation being 'resolved to spare no expense in order to render travelling by his conveyance safe, punctual and pleasant.'

How successful he was has not been recorded but this early 19th century venture did not presage the speedy establishment of a network of services so it was not until 1839 that evidence can be found of genuine urban public transport development. A notice from the *Leeds Mercury* early in that year gives details of a change in the town starting point of a horse bus service to the Three Horse Shoes at Headingley also recording that the fare at that time was sixpence. Growth by several private operators followed this but the lack of metalled road surfaces at that period severely limited the load which could be hauled and the typical two horse bus of the day had seats for only 12 to 15 passengers.

Similar problems had been experienced in America where the potential of the significant reduction in friction achieved by using a steel wheel on a steel rail for street travel had been realised before 1830. A smoother ride could be given and the same number of horses could handle a substantially greater payload. Even so in America growth was slow up to 1850, whilst the first experiment in Europe was not until 1853 when Alphonse Loubat was allowed to give a demonstration in Paris which was sufficiently successful that he was granted a concession to operate a regular service. Development continued to be slow, however, and it was 1870 before plans for street rail services were made on any significant scale.

In the meantime, using a mechanism for changing between flanged and flangeless wheels, William Joseph Curtis started operations over the lines of the Mersey Docks and Harbour Board in 1859. That body allowed other operators to copy him to such an extent that its goods trains were seriously disrupted and after some months the passenger services had to be stopped. More conventional developments were taking place across the River Mersey in Birkenhead where George Francis Train, an American, obtained permission to lay tracks from Woodside Ferry to Birkenhead Park. This was done using step rails which projected three quarters of an inch above the level of the road. Service started on 30 August 1860 but the difficulties created for other road users resulted in the line being relaid with flush grooved rails. Train then extended his activities to Liverpool, London, Darlington and the Potteries, but only in the latter were grooved rails substituted and a lasting and successful service operated.

Developments took place in other places in England and Parliament chose to regularise these through the Tramways Act of 1870 which had as its basis the assumption that local authorities would construct, or approve the construction of, tramways but would lease the working to private companies, although in abnormal cases special powers could be granted for corporations themselves to operate tramways. The leases were to operate initially for not more than twenty-one years, and after that period the local authority would be empowered to buy the system, the option thereafter being open at the end of each further seven year period.

Leeds was quick to take advantage of this and a 'Tramways Order Confirmation Act 1871' (dated 14 August) concerned the construction of tramways in Cardiff, Leeds and Yarmouth. The lines authorised in Leeds were:

| | | |
|---|---|---|
| 1. | Boar Lane to Kirkstall | (Star and Garter) |
| 2. | Boar Lane to Headingley | (Three Horse Shoes Inn) |
| 3. | Boar Lane to Chapeltown | (Queens Arms Hotel) |
| 4. | Boar Lane to Hunslet | (Crooked Billet Inn) |
| 5. | Duncan Street to Marsh Lane | (Shoulder of Mutton Inn) |

and these were all to be single track with passing loops.

One or two of the clauses in the Act are of interest, for instance Section 8 authorised the conveyance of 'passengers, animals, goods, materials and parcels' whilst Section 9 empowered the collection of

> tolls and charges not exceeding one penny per mile (fractions of mile equal one mile), but Promoters may charge threepence for any distance less than three miles.

A further clause gave the Board of Trade, following written protests from ratepayers and others within three years of the opening that the charges were unreasonable or that the company was charging more than twopence for distances not exceeding two miles, authority to re-examine the question of tolls.

Section 11 was a statutory demand about the running of workmen's cars as follows:

> The Promoters shall run carriages each way every morning in the week and every evening in the week (Sundays, Christmas Day and Good Friday always excepted) at such hours, not being later than seven in the morning or earlier than six in the evening respectively, for artisans, mechanics and daily labourers at tolls or charges not exceeding one halfpenny per mile (the Promoters nevertheless not being required to take any fares less than one penny). Provided that in case of complaint made to the Board of Trade of the hours appointed by the Promoters for the running of such carriages the said Board shall have power to fix and regulate the same from time to time.

Thus the Board of Trade had control over fares and certain aspects of the service to be provided.

Construction started in June 1871 when a gang of thirty men started work on Woodhouse Moor and soon after other gangs started in Boar Lane and Park Row. A contemporary report mentioned that it was hoped that the Kirkstall line, when built, would be used to move railway wagons to the various manufacturing premises along that road. The Headingley service began operation on 16 September 1871 over the 2 miles 7 furlongs to the Oak using double deck cars hauled by two or three horses, and the Kirkstall line followed at Easter, 1 April 1872, with similar cars and haulage, the route mileage being the same. The other lines authorised by the Act were not proceeded with at once, nor did the Headingley line reach its authorised limit until 1875.

A second Leeds Tramways Act, passed on 6 August 1872, was mainly concerned with regularising operations by incorporating the Leeds Tramways Company and authorising them to acquire tramways in the Borough of Leeds. The Promoters in the 1871 Act were named as Directors of the new company and an important provision was contained in Section 7 which extended the duration of the powers for construction of the remaining three lines until 1 August 1874.

Full use was made of this dispensation and no further routes were opened until 1874 when the remaining authorised sections began operation with horse traction as follows:

| | | |
|---|---|---|
| Hunslet | (1 mile 7 furlongs) | 2 March 1874 |
| York Road | (6 furlongs) | 29 August 1874 |
| Chapeltown | (2 miles 6 furlongs) | 14 November 1874 |

The York Road and Chapeltown routes were worked by one-horse single

**Plate 2** Leeds Tramways Company Ashbury built Eades 'reversible' double deck horse car No. 58 at the Woodman Inn, Headingley

*(Copyright Leeds City Transport)*

**Plate 3** Leeds Tramways Company Milnes single deck horse car at York Road terminus

*(Copyright Leeds City Transport)*

deckers and the Hunslet route by two or three horse double deckers. Details of all these cars are given in Appendix B.

The first act authorising extensions was given Royal Assent on 2 August 1877, the routes being from a junction with the Kirkstall line in Wellington Street to the Crown Inn at Wortley via Wellington Road (1 mile 5 furlongs), and from a junction with the Chapeltown line at the end of North Street for 5 furlongs along Meanwood Road. The Wortley line was single track with loops but the short Meanwood Road line began with a stretch of double line, the remainder being single. There had been considerable negotiation between the Tramways Company and the Corporation about the routes proposed, the corporation preferring to have an extension to the Star Inn at Wortley rather than the Company proposals for three short lines in the Hunslet area. The Corporation, being the Highway Authority, carried the day. The Meanwood line was opened on 16 July 1878 using small one-horse cars similar to those on the Chapeltown and York Road routes whilst the Wortley route opened in two stages on 1 January and 5 April 1879 with the usual two or three horse double deckers. This signified the end of expansion for a decade, apart from an extension to the Meanwood line in 1887 but the introduction of steam traction followed very quickly, probably as a direct result of early local developments in this field.

Experiments with steam traction for passenger carrying vehicles had been made in the early part of the nineteenth century involving self-propelled road rather than rail guided vehicles on the streets but without lasting success. Since that period vast strides had been made with railway steam engine design, especially in reliability, and railway style operation on street tramways was given thought. Consequently during 1876 steam tramway traction was introduced in Paris in March by an English company granted a concession, in Leicester from 27 March and on the Wantage Tramway in Berkshire from 1 August. These developments led the Leeds locomotive building firm of Kitson's to enter the steam tram engine business, the first public trial of one of their engines, actually built for overseas use, taking place on the Kirkstall–Hunslet section on 24 October 1877.

The Tramways Company must have been impressed because they decided to introduce steam traction and hired a Kitson engine which was delivered in 1880. The original engines had been equipped with vertical boilers but by the time the Leeds Company took delivery the design had been altered by adoption of a normal horizontal boiler and enlargement of the cylinders. The Board of Trade laid down stringent regulations about steam tram engines, the major points being that they should not emit visible smoke or steam and that the working parts should be enclosed above 4 inches from the ground as a guard against accidents from the side rods and motion. These requirements had a marked effect on the appearance of the engines, which usually looked like a very small single deck tram with a tall chimney towards one end and no visible wheels. To avoid emitting steam they had to be built with condensing equipment and to prevent the emission of smoke they burned coke, which, if cleaner, was certainly no less sulphurous than coal.

Being of considerably greater power than horses they were able to haul large double deck bogie cars, which had enclosed top decks but external stairs and up to 66 seats. Capacities such as this were not achieved by motor buses until the 30 foot long designs arrived in 1958, and full details are given in Appendix B. In Leeds steam working was introduced experimentally on the Wortley route on 17 June 1880 using the first Kitson engine alongside the horse cars. The Tramways Company was very satisfied with the experiment and quickly sought Board of Trade authority for steam operation over all its lines. The one Kitson engine continued, being supplemented in March and May 1881, by two more after which horse car working ceased on the Wortley line. These were on hire and hauled double deck horse cars until the first trailer cars specifically for steam haulage were purchased in 1882–3. The three Kitson engines, numbered 1 to 3, were a modified version of six then recently supplied for use in New Zealand.

Two further engines also numbered 1 and 2 were delivered, again on hire, on 1 January 1883 again locally built by Green's of Leeds to a design patented by Wilkinson of Wigan. The patent concerned a device in the firebox for superheating the exhaust steam instead of using the normal condensing pipes and the engines also had a crankshaft and cog-wheel drive. They were used on the Headingley line and were not successful for, in 1884, further enlarged Kitson engines were delivered and these replaced the Green engines, taking numbers 4–11. In January 1883 Kitson engines 1–3 were purchased, so that eleven were now in use. Six more similar but further enlarged Kitson were placed in service during 1886–7 and these had duplicated controls to allow normal operation in reverse thereby giving the driver a much better view of the road ahead, a very sensible arrangement which was not copied by other steam tram engine manufacturers. These took the numbers 13–18 and after their delivery full steam working was in operation on the Wortley and Headingley routes. Large numbers of these Kitsons engines were built for overseas use and one supplied to New Zealand in 1881 is preserved today in working order.

Tram engine No 12 was supplied by Greens in 1885 to their own design which was similar to an inside cylinder Kitson locomotive but with a Wilkinson style cab and a form of air exhaust condenser designed by the Falcon Company of Loughborough. Leeds tramways were subsequently to have a great deal of contact with this plant which in later years became the very well known Brush Electrical Engineering Company. Twelve further engines of this type were ordered and delivered between 1890 and 1894 to work new routes for which authority had been obtained, and the three original engines were withdrawn, so that twenty-five remained in use in 1894.

By 1888 further extensions of the system were considered desirable to serve developing areas and an Act in that year authorised two new lines, from the Chapeltown line at Sheepscar to Roundhay (the point now known as Oakwood at which the main entrance to Roundhay Park was then situated) and from the Meanwood Road route to Hyde Park via Woodhouse Street. The Roundhay route was constructed by the Corporation, completed in July 1889, and the Tramways Company provided a steam service on certain holiday days in August. However agreement could not be reached between the Tramways Company and the Corporation, the Tramways Company not having rolling stock and with only 3 years of the lease left no incentive to obtain any. Consequently no service ran for nearly two years. The Corporation received an offer to electrify the line and, having decided to accept it, did manage to agree with the Tramways Company to provide a steam service from 15 May 1891. The Tramways Company never operated the Woodhouse Street service.

The use of electricity for traction purposes dates from 1881 when Werner von Siemens started a public service in Berlin between Lichterfelde and the Anhalt Cadet School, about 1½ miles. This used the running rails as conductors and the obvious dangers of this prevented any widespread street developments on these principles. During the next few years much ingenuity was shown, especially in America, in solving this and other problems and a line using the familiar trolley pole was fully opened in Richmond, Virginia, by Frank Julian Sprague from 2 February 1888. This was an instantaneous success and showed the way for the great electric tramway growth which followed.

Third rail and battery cars operated at various places in England during the 1880s but the Roundhay route in Leeds was the first to use the overhead trolley system for current collection, being, as mentioned earlier, the subject of a separate concession. This was granted to William Graff-Baker, the representative of the Thomson-Houston Company of America, to electrify and operate the already constructed Roundhay line and also a new single track route along Harehills Road to Beckett Street. These were equipped with overhead wires supported between poles at either side of the road by 'span' wires, current being supplied by a generating station at about the half-way point. The Sheepscar-Roundhay section had a rather eventful opening ceremony on 29 October 1891, full service starting on 10 November 1891, the Harehills Road-Stanley Road section following the next day.

Six single deck cars were supplied by a New York company, to the standard design of John Stephenson, having six window bodies, curved clerestory roofs and canopies covering the whole platform, very similar to the New York horse cars in appearance. Each platform was accessible from both sides, an expanding wire gate being provided to close off that not in use. The cars weighed six tons, had seats for twenty-two passengers, with interior lighting by five incandescent lamps, and were powered by two fifteen horsepower motors. A contemporary report in *The Electrician* reads 'the fittings and fixtures are very handsome' and a little later that 'the cars are necessarily of the single deck type', showing that initially the idea of a double deck car taking current from an overhead line was hardly even considered. Contemporary newspaper cuttings record that these cars were entirely satisfactory in operation and comment upon their speedy operation in snow and mud – mention being made of speeds of twelve to fifteen miles per hour. Suggestions in other publications that a quickly resolved problem over interference with the telephone system and the eventual reconstruction by the Corporation show that this was an unsuccessful and insignificant experiment quite ignore that all European overhead current collection systems derived from it and that it ran for five years with general public approbation. Its centenary is that of an event of considerable technical and social significance.

The original concession to the Tramways Company, being for twenty-one years, was due to expire in August 1893, and they showed no interest in renewing it. In view of the impending end of their operations maintenance had been reduced to a minimum and concern was being expressed about the situation. The position matters had reached is highlighted by a report of a meeting of the Highways Committee (at that time responsible for tramways) at the end of January 1892 at which the minutes of its tramway sub-committee were read and approved. These included a resolution dealing with the condition of the Headingley tramway lines and requesting that an Inspector of the Local Government Board should be instructed to view the lines forthwith for the purpose of determining whether or not the traffic could, with safety to the public, be continued. A resolution was also confirmed to the effect that the Council be recommended, as the Local Authority under the 1870 Tramways Act, to pass a resolution under Section 43 of that Act, requesting the Leeds Tramways Company to sell to the Corporation their undertaking as authorised by the Leeds Tramways Orders of 1871.

The first resolution was implemented on Tuesday 1 March 1892 when Major General Hutchinson inspected the Headingley line, on foot for most of the distance, after which he was reported as saying he would have no hesitation in recommending to the Local Government Board that steam traction should cease on the Headingley route. He also expressed the view, not subsequently incorporated in his report, that the poor condition of the track could have been rectified by the Corporation's taking advantage of the clause in their agreement which gave them power to effect necessary repairs and charge the cost to the

**Plate 4** Leeds Tramways Company Kitson steam car No. 4 and Ashbury trailer No. 71 on the Headingley route

*(Copyright Leeds City Transport)*

**Plate 5** Leeds Tramways Company Greens steam car No. 28 and Milnes trailer No. 37 at Wortley

*(Copyright Yorkshire Post Newspapers)*

Tramways Company. His official report was published the following week, the main comments being that nothing but complete reconstruction of two and a half miles of tramway on an improved system would make its condition what it should be, that the Corporation were quite right in having refused to allow the Tramways Company to relay the tramway with a similar permanent way and that so long as engines were allowed to run it would go from bad to worse.

The discontinuance of steam working on the Headingley line was therefore decided upon and the Highways Committee gave the Tramways Company official notice to that effect. Some thought must have been given in advance to this probability because the Tramway's Manager undertook to recommend to his Board that steam working should be introduced on the Kirkstall line, the horse cars from that route being drafted to the Headingley line, and this was effected from the morning of Friday 11 March 1892. The Highways Committee was left with responsibility for seeing that the Headingley route track was put in good order.

So far as the second resolution was concerned, the position was, to say the least, confused. Section 43 of the 1870 Tramways Act dealt with the question of a Highway Authority taking over at the end of a concession but in 1893 Special Powers were still necessary for a municipal body to operate a tramway system. Although it was then ten years since Huddersfield Corporation had started operations themselves because they were unable to find anybody willing to operate their complete system, no general dispensation had been given to facilitate transfer from the companies to the municipalities. The problem with clause 43 was the valuation of the undertaking to be handed over and earlier difficulties had led to its being considered by the House of Lords, the resultant 'interpretation' confusing the issue even more. The simplest solution was arbitration!

Considerable public interest was voiced in the press, both in support of the Corporation's taking over and in support of new concessionaires. An alternative frequently suggested was to give Graff-Baker a new concession to operate the whole system, the idea being that this would include electrification, the other routes then being run as well and managed as effectively as the Roundhay line. Contemporary opinion was obviously impressed with the way the electric line was worked and hence there was a desire to see that form of traction extended.

The arbitration by Sir Douglas Galton KCB lasted from 25 to 28 July 1893 and the Tramway Company representation was led by Sir Richard Webster, Q.C., who opened by describing the extent of the undertaking quoting the gross track mileage, including access lines and depots, as 22 miles 3 furlongs 2.7 chains. Seven depots were referred to at Headingley, Chapeltown, Hunslet, Kirkstall, Wellington Street and Boar Lane with good stables and three hundred and fifty-eight horses. The operating stock was quoted, incorrectly, as twenty-five double-deck horse cars, fifteen single deck horse cars, twenty-four steam cars and twenty-five steam engines (see Appendix B). A lengthy discussion took place about the condition of the track, during which the General Manager, W. Wharam, was questioned and agreed that no repairs had been carried out on the Headingley route since 1884, that the Kirkstall line was not really fit for steam cars and that they were tearing it to pieces. There was a prolonged interchange about the way in which track repairs had been carried out and this included comments about the use of rails of one foot in length, of which Mr Wharam agreed some had been used. Agreement on a figure for the transfer was finally reached at £112,225, made up of £58,000 for track, £23,520 for land, depots and offices, £823 for fixed plant, £30,152 for loose plant, engines rolling stock harness etc. plus £6,589 for the arbitration. The Roundhay and Beckett Street lines were also valued at £15,232 and £5,098 respectively, these having been constructed by the Corporation. The transfer was effective from 2 February 1894 and the working continued under the Tramways Company General Manager, W. Wharam, who thus became the first Leeds Corporation General Manager. The Thomson-Houston concession continued for the electric lines, although Graff-Baker had by then left Leeds.

Action was taken to obtain the special powers required for a municipality to operate a tramway system and these were finally granted in 1896, by which time such restrictions had generally been removed.

The twenty-two years of company operation had not made any great impact on the majority of people, since the routes that had been opened ran to the pleasanter and more fashionable parts of the city. Of the places served by tram, Chapeltown, Headingley and Kirkstall were still villages separated from the city by open country, Hunslet was similarly separated and at that time growing very rapidly, and the Wortley route served an area also being extensively developed. Although the various tramways Bills required workmen's cars to be run in the morning before seven and in the evening after five or six, few such morning cars were operated and first cars were in most cases after eight in the morning. The notable exceptions were the independently managed electric routes which started at 6 a.m. Thus all the workers must have lived within walking distance of their work and transport development had remained restricted to the wealthier areas which were thought to be the source of adequate revenue. Had this policy continued, the great changes of the next forty years could not have taken place.

The introduction of rail borne public transport vehicles had to some extent mitigated the transport problems arising from the poor condition of the roads, which within the city were cobbled and elsewhere often unsurfaced, most of the major work of tar spraying, chipping and making 'public' not being undertaken until the 1920s. As described earlier, horse, and later steam, haulage of trams had enabled much larger loads to be conveyed, but both of these were very slow. The electrification of the Roundhay route had pointed the way forward but the impetus obviously had to be seized by an organisation other than the Tramways Company and take over by a modernisation and expansion committed Corporation provided the necessary opportunity.

CHAPTER 2

# The Corporation take-over – electrification

The tramway system continued under the control of the Highways Committee, with William Wharam remaining as Manager. An immediate change was from 10 March 1894 when steam cars began working through from Wortley to Chapeltown, turning at Leopold Street, but otherwise attention was focussed on the best ways to extend and improve the system. The Highways Committee appointed Tramways sub-committees from time to time, an important occasion being 12 November 1894, after which it was decided that a policy decision must be made on the form of traction to be adopted for future development.

There was considerable public pressure for extensions to the system, of which the following letter to the *Leeds Mercury* dated 19 January 1894 is typical:

> In any new arrangement made in our tramway system, is it too much to hope that the Roundhay line may be extended to the Canal Gardens? From the present terminus to the Mansion is about one and a half miles and to walk this distance both ways is too much for anyone with young children, and spoils all the pleasure. If the line was extended, would it not enable the Corporation to sell some of the land adjoining and so relieve the rates?
>
> Signed, 'Ratepayer.'

The Highways Committee was alive to the benefits to be obtained from extending the system and therefore requested the City Engineer to prepare a report on the various systems of tramway haulage, also sending the sub-committee on an extensive tour to inspect and report upon the systems in other towns and cities. The City Engineer's report was ready in January 1895 and was a very thorough work. In it all the systems adopted in Great Britain (horse, steam, cable, electric) and also those available but not adopted in Great Britain on a commercial basis were examined. The latter systems used oil engines, gas engines and compressed air engines and the owners of two of the gas engine systems, one French and the other in use at Dessau in Germany, were prepared to take leases of the Hunslet and Kirkstall routes, because of the easiness of the gradients. To use the system on two routes only was obviously most undesirable and as the other sections included, by inference, gradients too steep for gas engine operation, its practicability for use in Leeds was discounted. Compressed air cars were used in Nantes but the cars where very heavy and the closeness of the axles was said to create a continual see-saw motion, damaging to the rails and disagreeable to the passengers. A newer system designed by M.Conti was available and although it was conceded that this would be the best such system, it was considered the administration losses would be so great as to outweigh any advantages.

So far as the other systems in use were concerned, Mr Hewson's views were simple and clearly set out as follows:

> If it were not now a matter of certainty that both horses and steam cost more than either of the other systems (excepting the accumulator) it is quite clear that the present system is played out. For as to horses, their work on heavy gradients is too severe, if not inhuman, they occupy, wear, obstruct and foul the roads; they are slow in speed; it is impossible to keep a sufficient reserve of them for fete days; and they necessitate the employment of so great a number of workmen that the system is more liable to suffer from strikes than any other system. As to the steam engine, its street obstruction, its steam, smoke, smell, dust, noise, and ugliness utterly condemn it where any other form of mechanical traction (except a gas engine which is its own cousin) even at a slightly higher cost could be got.

These comments effectively disposed of everything except electric traction and cable haulage and the Engineer went on to argue the financial case between these two methods of operation. It was judged necessary to recondition the whole of the track and the cost of this was estimated at £183,946, or £5,256 per mile, which was thought to compare very favourably with the cost of £5,155 per mile for the best and most recently laid track in the city. The importance of costs was related to the fact that the Tramways had for the most part been, and it was expected would in the future be, renewed out of capital. After giving a thorough review of the total service in 1894, including trains and public and private buses, the Engineer acknowledged that a better service was required and recommended that a basic seven and a half minute headway should be provided to the farthest extent of each route, augmented by short workings to give a three and three-quarters minute headway over the busier sections of each route. These 'short' workings were to terminate at Reginald Terrace (Chapeltown Road), Waterloo Road (Kirkstall), Wellington Road (Wortley) and Hyde Park (Headingley). To run this service would necessitate doubling the track on the whole system except Beckett Street (still to be constructed) and the cost of the additional facilities to do this with the existing horse and steam traction, excluding the track, was estimated at £265,884. The service over the central area was to be one and seven eights minutes between Sheepscar and Park Row and this proved to be significant in the final decision.

Estimates were prepared of the costs for introducing electric and cable traction, based on costs and declared results from undertakings using these modes of traction. The estimate for adoption of the cable system was £428,922, excluding running track, and for overhead electric £378,499, again excluding track. The electric conduit system was also examined but was discounted as the cost was £137,760 more than for the overhead system. An assessment was made of the annual costs of running the proposed improved service by each method as follows:

| | |
|---|---|
| Horse & Steam | £117,292 |
| Cable | £101,819 |
| Electric Overhead | £ 90,072 |

and the electric overhead was thus cheaper on running costs by £11,747 per annum as well as £50,423 on capital outlay. All these estimates assumed that an equivalent service would yield similar revenue irrespective of mode of traction.

The report contained a lengthy summarised list of the advantages and otherwise of the electric and cable systems as follows:

Advantages of electric over cable:

(1) No central slot to catch horses' shoes or bicycle wheels and only two rails instead of three for wheels to skid against;
(2) All power generated at the electric station is utilised, whereas by cable threequarters of the total power generated is used for hauling the cable, however few the number of cars running may be;
(3) Electric cars may run at varying speeds and so make up for any loss of time, but not so the cable;
(4) The cable mode of construction involves repairs and interference with the traffic of the streets which is not the case with electric;
(5) Electric cars can accommodate themselves to street traffic, whilst cable cars cannot as their speed is regulated by the cable and they cannot move backwards;
(6) A broken or blocked cable stops the whole route, both up and down, and the cars have to be hauled by some supplementary power off the streets, and the cable service on the route (up and

**Plate 6** View of Briggate 1880–90 showing a double deck horse car of the Leeds Tramways Company passing the cab rank

*(Copyright Yorkshire Post Newspapers)*

**Plate 7** City Square, probably 1901, with a single deck horse car proceeding towards Boar Lane and an open top electric car proceeding towards Park Row

*(Copyright Yorkshire Post Newspapers)*

down) is suspended until repaired, which must be a considerable length of time; whereas a breakage in the electric wire is purely local and as the motor cars can move either backwards or forwards the service can be continued by using the opposite track for both traffics or changing cars at the point of fracture;
(7) Less likelihood of traffic being stopped for renewing of wire leads than of cables. No new wires have yet had to be fixed in Roundhay Road, though they have been up three years, whereas cables have to be renewed every year, though by careful daily examination this is often done at night;
(8) Brake power failing on a decline, control is maintained over the electric car by reversing the motors. Cable cars cannot reverse but must go with the cable or run away;
(9) Cars lit by electricity are more comfortable and convenient;
(10) In case of being superseded by another system the materials and work totally lost would be much less in the electric system than with the cable system;
(11) The electric overhead system has a greater field of improvement open to it in regard to cost than the cable system has.

Advantages of cable over electric
(1) No unsightly poles, overhead cross wires or trolley wire along whole length of each track
(2) No sparking at trolley or car wheels to frighten horses
(3) Less wear of metals, the load being less and a rolling load as compared with the grinding load of an electric car
(4) More silent on the road, no buzzing of motors or rattle of gearing
(5) No danger from falling overhead wire
(6) A very large number of extra cars can be put upon a route to meet an emergency at a very slight increase in cost.

Adding the greater advantages of electric over cable to the already strong financial arguments, Hewson's conclusion was that the overhead electric system was the answer. It was also considered that for sound profitability the cable system required a 1⅞ minute headway overall, and as this was only proposed over the very small central area in Leeds, with substantial lengths having a 7½ minute headway, cable operation could not be seen as being profitable. He made certain recommendations to minimise the unsightliness of support poles and concluded as follows:

> I am of the opinion that the Electric Overhead system of tramway haulage is certainly to-day and more certainly for the future the best system for the city of Leeds.

Whilst Hewson was preparing his report, the Highways Sub-Committee (Tramways) had visited Birmingham, Darlaston, Newcastle, Edinburgh, Glasgow, Brixton, Croydon, The Isle of Man, Brussels, Paris and Le Havre, examined all the systems in use, and obtained comparative costs. When they returned they considered the Engineer's report and stated that they had come to the conclusion that the existing mixed horse and steam working should be superseded, that oil, gas and compressed air were considered impracticable and that, having regard to the many routes, involving varying requirements for service frequency without really steep gradients, electrical traction was the most suitable.

The Sub-Committee's report was carefully prepared to demonstrate that the decision was based on the established facts. Thus they were careful to show they had given consideration to the benefits of cable operation in dense or on very steep routes and expressed the view that the conduit electric system would be better through the City Centre from the Dispensary in North Street to Queen Street in Wellington Street and as far as the top of Park Row. The City Engineer was asked to prepare a supplementary report, which was speedily produced (4 February 1895) wherein he estimated the additional capital cost would be £10,183, and the additional annual cost £2,230. He also raised the problem of changeover from one system to the other, expressing his doubts as follows:

> Unless very effective automatic machinery can be made to do the work, there will necessarily be, with a service so frequent as one and seven eighths minutes, an interference with the traffic in passing the cars from one system to another, and there would be ten of such changing places.

After production of this supplementary report the question was again considered by the Sub-Committee, it was agreed to discard any idea of conduit for the central area and a special Council Meeting was called to deal with the reports and recommendations. The final decision to electrify the system was taken on 15 October 1895 and a local election having provided a change of committee chairman in November 1895 it was decided to implement the electrification policy as quickly as practicable. The Kirkstall–Roundhay section was selected as the first route to be dealt with and an Act was sought to provide the necessary powers and also permit substitution of forms of traction.

The need to expand the system was too pressing to wait for electrification and the Acts of 1896 and 1897 authorised a large number of new routes, as well as some extensions to the existing ones. Apart from an extension along York Road, the first group of extensions were to the Wellington Road route and were steam worked, together with Victoria Road, also operated by steam cars as an extension to the

**Plate 8** Original Sheepscar–Roundhay electric car No. 80 at Stanley Road terminus

*(Courtesy Leeds Reference Library)*

**Plate 9** The first Leeds City Transport electric cars for the Kirkstall–Roundhay section, No. 6 at Kirkstall Abbey terminus

*(Copyright Yorkshire Post Newspapers)*

Woodhouse Street line. During 1900, however, new routes were opened with horse traction along Armley Road, to Malvern Road (Beeston route), along Elland Road, and in 1901 along Whitehall Road. Steam extensions were made possible by the purchase in 1897 of two additional engines from Greens, having Burrell condensers, numbered 29 and 30 at a cost of £700 each, together with release of units from the Kirkstall section by electrification. As a result of the other openings the number of horses increased from the three hundred and fifty-eight taken over in 1894 to a maximum of five hundred and ninety-three in 1900, while the total number of horse and steam trailer cars increased from sixty-eight in 1896 to eighty-six in 1899. The twenty-three new horse trailer cars were built by Milnes and the double deckers were very like the new electric cars, although a bit shorter, whilst the single deckers were similar to the previous ones purchased by the Tramways Company. Thus since the decision to electrify had been taken the size of the problem had grown, there being fifty-eight route miles of which only seven had been converted.

These seven miles were the Kirkstall-Roundhay section on which work was pressed forward rapidly after contracts had been let in June 1896. The work included replacement of much of the permanent way with rails of 100lb. per yard weight as well as all the overhead equipment. The British Thomson Houston Company, clearly not going to enjoy any involvement in extension of the electric system, gave notice at the end of June 1896 to end their operations. The last electric car ran on 31 July 1896, and a Briggate–Oakwood steam service started on 1 August. No doubt the Corporation were suited by notice to terminate the agreement being given since it facilitated the electrical reconstruction work. The Harehills Road-Stanley Road section had no service until the through steam service to the Corn Exchange via Beckett Street started on 25 April 1898.

It had been thought initially that certain of the original BTH overhead equipment between Sheepscar and Oakwood might be incorporated but it was finally decided it was obsolete and complete renewal was authorised. The span wire method of overhead support was supplanted by side poles with long bracket arms carrying two wires close together just left of the road centre from Sheepscar towards Roundhay, which looked like a single trolley-bus line. Centre 'T' bracket poles used at Harehills and in the city centre were an obstruction in the centre of the road which cannot have been too popular. An extension was made from Oakwood to the Canal Gardens at Roundhay as well as a short one from the Star and Garter to Kirkstall Abbey.

To operate the new frequencies over this line twenty-five new double deck, open top, four-wheeled electric cars were ordered, for completion by Messrs. Greenwood and Batley at their works in Armley Road. The bodies were built by Milnes of Birkenhead with four side windows having 'Tudor Arch' tops and they were without canopies. The cars were mounted on Peckham cantilever trucks supplied by R. W. Blackwell of London but it was stated at the time that Brill trucks would be used on some future cars for comparative purposes. These cars took the numbers 1–25, the horse and steam trailer cars having those numbers being re-numbered (see Appendix B). Trailer working was continued, eleven new trailer cars being supplied by Milnes and Brush to work with the electrics, and with these new vehicles the Roundhay route re-opened on 2 August 1897, cars working through between Roundhay and Kirkstall Abbey, which they continued to do until 3 April 1954. During 1898 the former Thomson-Houston cars were purchased by the Corporation and converted into trailer cars, together with a Brush built open sided trailer which had been acquired by the Thomson-Houston Company in 1896.

The results of this first conversion were all that had been hoped for and confirmed the wisdom of the council's decision to make the change. It was therefore decided to electrify the rest of the system as quickly as possible, although the next sections altered, Sheepscar–Chapeltown and City Square–Headingley were not completed until 3 January 1900. The remainder of the pioneer route from Harehills to Stanley Road was altered from 2 June 1900, sharing the section from the bottom of York Road with the York Road cars which were electrically worked from 6 June 1900. It was from this latter date that Kirkgate was made the inward line and New York Road the outward. The Beckett Street section remained single and was eventually one of the last single line sections in use. Conversion of the remaining routes, including those sections opened by the Corporation was pushed ahead, an observation being made in the 1901 report that contracts let would complete the elimination of horse and steam traction, the last regular horse cars running on the Whitehall Road route on the 13 October 1901 and the last steam cars on the Armley route on 1 April 1902. The tables at the end of this book set out the openings and closures of all the routes and summarise in chronological order the advent of the various types of traction. Some significant figures show that the horse and steam extensions were well justified, but that the electric working transformed the situation.

Thus in the year ended 30 June 1894 a total of 1,109,775 car miles were run and 8,412,395 passengers carried over twenty-two miles of route, the Corporation having increased the annual mileage, other than electric, operated from 906,943 to 1,050,183. By the year ended 25 March 1900 car miles had reached 2,664,154, passengers carried 27,634,105 over 58 route miles of track, and a net profit of £6167 was made. After the first wave of electrification extensions, by the year ended 31 March 1906, the same figures were 7,126,185 car miles, 69,634,126 passengers, 96 route miles and £51,500 net profit. The

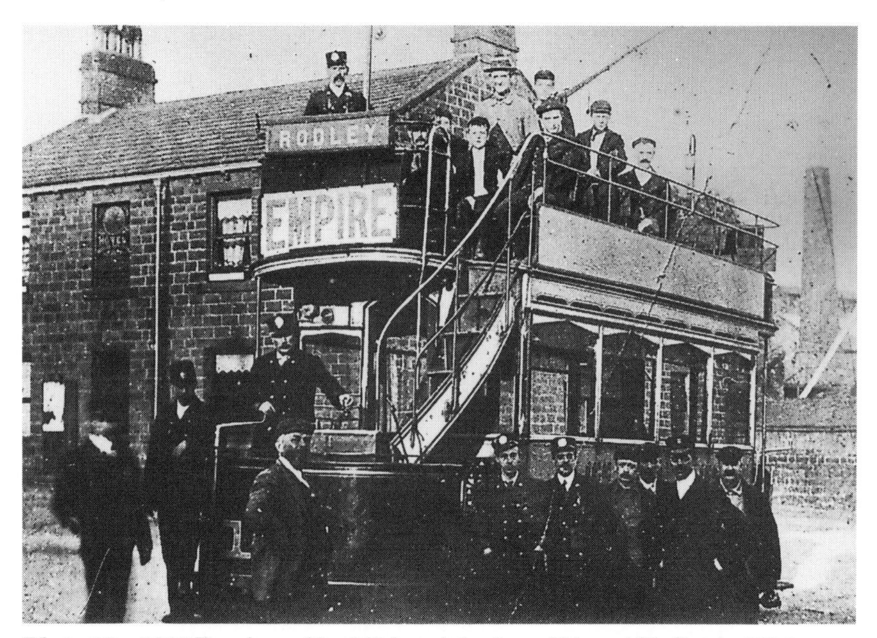


**Plate 10** 1899 Brush car No. 166 in original condition at Rodley in 1906

*(Copyright Leeds City Transport)*

**Plate 11** 1900 Dick Kerr car No. 280 at Kirkstall Road works about 1912 showing the Maley platform brake wheel and track shoes

*(Copyright Leeds City Transport)*

success of the electric system is further demonstrated by the fact that without any major increases in route mileage, by the year ended 25 March 1909 car mileage was up to 7,828,794 and 76,215,618 passengers were carried, although the net profit that year was only £47,556.

To make possible this growth the electric car fleet had risen from the original twenty-five motor cars and eighteen trailers, to two hundred and seventy motor cars, although trailer working had been abandoned.

Leeds electric trams have always been noted for the variety of types and the two hundred and twenty purchased between 1899 and 1902 were no exception. The first batch of fifty were Brush built and were very similar to the original Milnes cars also having 'Tudor Arch' windows to the saloon. These cars took the numbers 133–182 as the numbers between 26 and 132 were still mainly in use for horse, steam and electric trailer cars. Two additional cars were also delivered by Brush about this time, very similar but having 'round arch' windows and these received the numbers 85 and 90. Together with Nos. 150–9 they were equipped with magnetic track brakes, all twelve being used on the hilly Beeston route after it opened early in 1901, along with five very similar cars purchased in 1900 also fitted with magnetic track brakes. These were known as 'Liverpool' cars and had run there for a short time as Nos. 464–8, but how they came to Leeds is not quite certain. They were given numbers 44, 46, 55, 79 and 83. Full details of all cars are given in Appendix B.

During 1900 more 'odd' cars were taken into stock. The first was a single decker, given the number 49, which had been built by J. G. Brill and shown at the 1900 Tramways and Light Railways Exhibition. It was described as 'convertible', having side panels which could be raised to make it open sided. In Leeds it was generally restricted to the short Whitehall Road route on which its convertible attributes were of minimum advantage. A second was number 52, a Brush bodied five window round arch open top double decker on Brill maximum traction bogies which had been used for experiments in Beckett Street with the Anderson surface contact system. It was later mounted on a Brill truck and later still on a 'long wheelbase' truck. The final additions in 1900 were made by the conversion of former trailer cars, six Milnes built numbered 98–103 and five Brush built numbered 128–132. At the same time the former Thomson Houston cars were converted to salt cars and trailer working ceased for passenger service. All the four-wheeled double deckers in service at this time had four-window bodies, the rebuilt Milnes trailers having Tudor Arch window tops and the Brush ones round.

In 1901 one hundred new cars were placed in service, numbered 183 to 282 and built by Dick Kerr with canopied platforms, reversed stairs, and three-window bodies in which fan-light ventilation to the lower saloon was introduced. They were mounted on Brill trucks as suggested for comparative purposes when the first electric cars were delivered and were followed in 1902 by fifty very similar cars from Brush, reverting to Peckham trucks. These took a variety of numbers, made spare as a result of withdrawal of various old trailer cars as follows 27–32, 34, 39, 40, 42, 43, 45, 47, 48, 50, 51, 56, 57, 58, 67–70, 74–78, 80, 82, 84, 86, 87, 91–97 and 104–113. All but twelve had Westinghouse Magnetic Track brakes.

Open top cars left quite a lot to be desired for all year round operation in British weather and experiments were soon made with top deck covers on some of the canopied cars. Brush 1902 cars 51 and 82 were the first, being supplied with a 'convertible' affair, built by Milnes, in which the ends were solid but the centre was a canvas cover (striped) over a metal frame such that the cover could be folded up. The local Portuguese Vice-Consul, J. A. deMacedo was involved with, if not responsible for, the design. Two Dick Kerr cars were fitted with permanent top covers of the very typical British balcony pattern having four drop windows but no fan-light ventilators. These were much more successful and by 1906 all fifty 1902 cars had been equipped as well as fifty of the 1901 Dick Kerr cars. One of the 1902 cars, No. 94, was seen by a Sunderland corporation deputation and this standard top cover impressed them so much that they built a similar one for their car No. 29, the only information from which this was done being a photograph. In describing this incident S. A. Staddon observes that the origin of the photograph was not disclosed, but comparison of photographs of the two types of car highlights the similarities.

Twenty-five further Brush cars were supplied in 1904 differing from the 1902 ones in having Brush trucks and standard spiral stairs and all had Westinghouse magnetic track brakes. They entered service fitted with standard top covers and took up the remaining spare numbers, except 115–26, i.e. 26, 33, 35–38, 41, 53, 54, 59–66, 71–73, 81, 88, 89, 114, 127. These were the last cars obtained by Leeds to an outside body-builder's standard design and from then until 1926 all new cars were built by the Corporation, whilst after that year any built by contractors were to Leeds designs.

The first major phase of electrification and expansion lasted until the middle of 1906 by which time all the major routes had been opened along part of their ultimate length. The termini were all at the city boundary or the extent of housing development, except for the Rothwell route on which Corporation cars ran throughout over West Riding Company's tracks to balance West Riding cars working into the centre of Leeds from Wakefield over Corporation tracks from Hunslet (Thwaite Gate). This arrangement was subject to an agreement dated 6 June 1905 but through working started on 1 June 1905. West Riding cars had worked a Thwaite Gate–Rothwell service from mid December 1904. A section of 1 in 15 gradient in Wood Lane, Rothwell, required the use of track braked cars which Leeds provided and the West Riding Company never acquired. At this time the Dewsbury Road route ended at Cross Flatts, the Belle Isle route at Balm Road bridge, the York Road routes at Killingbeck Toll and the Otley Road route at Headingley. The Balm Road and York Road routes had recently been extended, while the Rodley route had recently been opened from Bramley Town End.

Statistically there was now no doubt of the wisdom of the 1895 decision. Car mileage had increased seven times and annual revenue had risen from £57,000 to £312,000, while the cost per car mile had remained fairly static – on the small Roundhay system in 1893 it was 5.54d, in 1906 it was 5.26d for the much larger system – with net profits averaging about £50,000 per annum, much of which was being used to relieve the rates. The buoyancy of business, together with a wish to encourage short distance traffic, led to the introduction in 1905 of halfpenny fares and with this incentive added to the vastly improved frequencies operated and much earlier morning journeys since electrification, over an extended system, a position had been reached where most people were riding where they had formerly walked, seventy million passengers being carried in 1906. This was what had been anticipated when the electrification decision was taken.

The preceding era had been one in which many other civic decisions had been notably sound and very obviously taken with a view to future growth of the city. The Water Company was purchased in 1862 and the Washburn Valley Reservoirs built, with a capacity well beyond the needs of the time, which gave an adequate water supply for many future years. The Sewage Works at Knostrop were laid out and commissioned with such foresight that at the present no major extension has been necessary and land remains available for any expansion in the foreseeable future. A beginning was made before 1900 in clearing away insanitary houses and widening streets, although on a very limited scale, and the movement did not gain any real impetus until about 1920.

Similar imagination had been used in considering recreational matters and when the fourteen hundred acres of Roundhay Park were offered for sale in 1872, the Corporation bought six hundred and sixteen for £139,000. This has been considerably developed over the years, a notable addition completed in 1907 being the Bathing Pool at the bottom of the Waterloo Lake waterfall which has now been demolished. This lake, up to sixty feet deep, is so called because it was completed in the year of the Battle of Waterloo (1815), after ten years work and at a cost of £20,000. Kirkstall Abbey also came on the market and the city was able to acquire it for £10,000 through the generosity of Colonel North, born in Leeds, but then living in Kent. This too has been consolidated over the years and although black rather than the more mellow stone colours of some of the country ruins, is now a notably preserved monument.

A very important influence in Leeds after 1856 was the development of the ready made garment industry. In that year Barran opened a small factory, using a few of the new sewing machines which had been invented in 1851 by Singer. Mechanised cutting followed quickly in 1858, when a band saw used by a local firm for cutting wood veneers was adapted for cutting several layers of cloth. Soon after this the idea of breaking manufacture down into its separate parts was tried so that unskilled workers could more easily be trained and from this point the industry grew, most particularly in Leeds, which soon became known as the world centre of the ready made clothing industry. In the first years of this century the great westward movement of East European Jews occurred and many reached Leeds, considerable numbers filling the employment need in the clothing factories and by 1907 there were twenty-five thousand in the city.

There had been growth in other industries following the Industrial Revolution and, as in other areas of the country, this, coupled with the Enclosure movement in Agriculture caused a migration from country to town and city. The level of real wages rose during the period 1871 to 1901 in the ratio of one hundred to one hundred and sixty-five, so that the spending capacity of most people was greatly increased. The same period had also seen a great growth in the immediate urban area to accommodate these new city-dwellers. Much of the housing was in streets at right-angles to the main roads and was 'back-to-back', that is to say that each house had only one door and one outside wall. This method of construction allowed large numbers of people to be housed in relatively small areas, although even by the early 1900s many of these areas had become very mean, and George Bernard Shaw made his well known remark that Leeds 'ought to be burned down' after travelling along Kirkstall Road, which was the main artery of one of the most extensive areas of such development.

The tramway system had thus been developed at a time particularly suited to its success. The increased spending capacity enabled people to afford to use public transport; the new factories, by concentrating places of work, required a higher proportion of people to make a journey to work; the tramway system enabled them to make that journey from the areas of new housing; the fact that the population was dense enabled the tramway to operate in ideal conditions at increasingly low fares, which in turn further increased the demand. Effective public transport was now established in the immediate urban area of the city and the next phase of development saw its projection to adjoining urban areas.

CHAPTER 3

# Further expansion – Leeds built cars

Two interesting events took place during the summer of 1905, the first being that the new Balm Road tram route displaced the last city centre horse bus service from Lower Briggate to Hunslet Carr, the last trip being on 1 June. The press report of this last departure refers to a new West Riding tram passing en route for Wakefield, the inaugural day for that service also, and to badinage between the drivers. The second event arose out of the election of Mr. Hamilton, the General Manager, to the Presidency of the Municipal Tramways Association. At the ceremony on 13 July, he expressed the view that motor buses had a future as feeders to tramways in the way certain horse buses had been and reported that two would start in Leeds 'next month' in conjunction with the Headingley and Wortley trams. He said they would have garden seats on the top deck similar to the up-to-date tramcars and be powered by 30 h.p. engines. The first motor bus route, in fact, began operation on 31 March 1906 between Headingley and Adel, so that Leeds was among the first undertakings to operate motor buses. They also began running as an extension to the Wortley trams in 1908, displacing the last horse buses in Leeds, which were operated by the Corporation.

Extension of the system was sought by people in most districts not served, although not always with unanimity, Whitkirk being an example. There was a great deal of controversy in the local press about the necessity, or wisdom, dependent on the viewpoint, of extending the system, a number of people writing letters to the press suggesting that there was already an adequate service of trains from Crossgates railway station. One pungent comment about this was that the people who were not in favour generally lived at the end of Whitkirk near the station and would not appreciate the position at the other end of the village to which the extension was proposed. Another case was the proposed line from the Parish Church to Knostrop Road via East Street, for which powers were obtained in 1906. Deputations urging construction went to the Town Hall more than once about this route and although powers were renewed a number of times, the line was never built. The General Manager himself advised one deputation in December 1908 that it was 'not felt to be necessary as the proposed route was nowhere longer than a quarter of a mile from an existing route and it would only run in competition'.

The next phase of the expansion, therefore, concerned what might now be called 'interurban' lines which, by virtue of the Tramways Act relating to Highways Authorities, had to be built and operated by agreement with the adjacent towns and boroughs. Leeds cars had first operated outside the boundary to an adjoining town from 1 June 1905 when through working to Rothwell began over the West Riding Company's tracks balanced by through working between Wakefield (Sandal) and Leeds Corn Exchange by West Riding cars over Leeds Corporation tracks from Thwaite Gate. Other adjacent towns pressed the Leeds management to enter into agreements with them to provide tram services and the first route opened under such an arrangement was that from Stanningley Bottom to Pudsey on which cars began running on 4 June 1908.

Stanningley Bottom was also the point at which passengers for Bradford changed cars and the undesirability of this was recognised. The first suggestion to facilitate through working was from Leeds and was to provide an additional rail along the whole route. This was countered by the Manager of the Bradford undertaking, C. J. Spencer, who, with his Assistant J. W. Dawson, designed an axle sleeve which would enable cars to operate on both the four foot gauge Bradford system and the four foot eight and a half inch Leeds tracks. The sleeve permitted the wheels to move along the axle as the car travelled over a short length of tapered track. A Peckham truck was adapted and after extensive tests was placed under Bradford car No. 124. A length of tapered track was laid at Stanningley Bottom over which No. 124 made an experimental trip on the night of 22 January 1907 from Thornbury to Armley Branch Road and back with both General Managers aboard. Further tests were made, a press report dated 17 April 1907 referring to the Leeds and Bradford Transport Committees inspecting the device at Thornbury depot, after which car No. 124 began a month's public service trial on 22 April 1907, the success of which led to inauguration of a regular one-car service on 24 September 1907.

A press report of 10 August 1908 indicated that the Board of Trade had agreed to a full service and the two undertakings began equipping ten cars each. Leeds chose cars of the 1902 Brush batch, on Peckham trucks, Nos. 87 and 104–112. Bradford also selected Brush cars built in 1902 but fitted them additionally with new top covers of their own design and construction, the numbers being 72, 76, 78, 93, 110, 111, 116, 118 and 127, whilst 124 received a similar top cover soon afterwards. Everything was ready by June and on 7 June 1909 inaugural cere-

**Plate 12** 1902 Brush car No. 82 showing the first experimental top cover fitted in 1903 in the open and closed positions

*(Copyright Leeds City Transport)*

monies took place, when cars were driven over the tapered track, a civic luncheon was held at Bradford Town Hall and the two decorated cars ran for the rest of the day without passengers. The full public service started on 9 June 1909.

Bradford and West Riding cars now ran into Leeds but no other through tram workings were introduced into Leeds nor into Bradford, although proposals for additional workings there using gauge changing equipment were made after the success of the Leeds working.

The next opening outside the boundary was to Morley and this route had quite a long history before cars started running. Powers for construction of tramways in Morley, Ardsley, Gildersome and Drighlington were obtained in 1901 by the British Electric Traction Company, which never exercised them, although, as is well known, it built and successfully operated many miles of tramway all over the country, including other parts of Yorkshire. The powers were then purchased by the Leeds and Bradford District Tramways Company but it too failed to take advantage of them and in the Autumn of 1910 they were purchased by Morley Corporation which immediately began negotiations with Leeds. There was no more delay and the Churwell route was quickly extended reaching Morley Fountain Street by 5 July 1911, Tingley Mill by 20 October 1911 and Bruntcliffe by 1 January 1912. The line was single with passing loops, controlled by a patent signalling device. The route included a length of 1 in 11 gradient on Churwell Hill which was the third and last steep section on the system, the others being Beeston Hill (1 in 10) and Whitecote Hill (1 in 8) on the Rodley route.

There had also been pressure for a number of years from Horsforth, Rawdon, Yeadon and Guiseley for a tramway extension and this was eventually opened in three sections between 1909 and 1915, the latter being the last section opened by Leeds outside the City Boundary, so that at that time the system reached its furthest point from the city centre. Extension of this route was campaigned for by Otley and Burley residents but the economics were not encouraging and before anything positive was done developments on the Whitehall Road route changed the picture.

Powers for an extension along Whitehall Road to Farnley had been available for some time and the residents were pressing for a service. The Tramways Department Management were not satisfied that this route would be a worthwhile proposition but had heard of the new 'trackless' trams (or trolley buses as they are known to-day) then running on the continent and sent a deputation to inspect the various systems. Three variants were examined, the principal differences being in the methods of current collection and of keeping the positive and negative shoes separate. The 'Filovia' system was examined in Milan, current collection being by a pair of wheels for each wire, pressed upward by normal trolley booms, while the Mercedes-Stoll system in

Vienna utilised a pair of wheels riding above the wires, held down by a weight, and connected to the car by wires. The third system was being used in Germany, at Mühlhausen (now Mulhouse), having been devised by Max Schliemann using normal trolley booms but with a pair of sliding shoes rather than wheels. The deputation considered that all the vehicles demonstrated satisfactory performance and manoeuvreability but they foresaw difficulty with the Mercedes-Stoll system in the event of the collector wheels becoming dislodged. It was stated two men with poles had considerable difficulty in replacing them.

It was decided that an experiment with trackless vehicles should be made on the Farnley route to see whether it provided a cheaper solution for serving less densely populated areas and a Bill was put forward to have a route from Wortley tram terminus through New Blackpool to Lawns Lane near Farnley Fireclay Works. This was soon amended to be City Square to New Farnley, it being thought that the existing powers would permit operation of trackless as well as rail guided trams. In October 1910, after work had begun, it was reported that there would be delay because the existing powers did not authorise trackless operation. The Corporation asked for a special waiver to allow work to continue, as, amongst other things, it would provide work for the unemployed, but although the Board of Trade agreed to see a deputation, it did not agree to the special waiver, promising, however, to obviate any undue delay in dealing with the necessary Bill.

Powers were eventually granted, Leeds being one of the first Municipal undertakings to obtain them in a Bill dated 28 November 1910, being described as 'an act to empower the Lord Mayor, Aldermen and citizens of Leeds to provide omnibuses worked by electricity and to construct a street and for other purposes.' The anticipated costs were given; for provision of vehicles, £5,500, and for provision of the electrical equipment and of other works necessary for working trolley vehicles, £9,000. The Corporation was expressly prevented from manufacturing trolley buses, presumably for sale since they built a number for their own use at Kirkstall Road works. It was stated that trolley vehicles should not be deemed to be light locomotives or motor cars within the terms of the Highways Acts.

Thereafter work was pressed forward so that an official opening was able to be held on 21 June 1911, the public service starting immediately afterwards with two single deck vehicles numbered 501 and 502, each capable of operation by one man. The original intention had been to start the ceremonial run at City Square but at the last minute it was decided to start in Whitehall Road to try and avoid congestion from the crowd expected in City Square. When the first car returned it was found that a number of guests, not being advised of the change, had been left behind and the crowd congestion in City Square was not avoided. Bradford also had an official ceremony in the morning but, having only

**Plate 13** The Briggate/Boar Lane crossroads about 1910 with Dick Kerr car No. 204 waiting to move out of Briggate

*(Courtesy Yorkshire Post Newspapers)*

**Plate 14** An unidentified Dick Kerr car decorated as a recruiting vehicle in 1914, with destination 'Berlin'. Leeds had a long tradition of decorated cars, right up to 1955.

*(Copyright Yorkshire Post Newspapers)*

one car of the two required for the public service available and also not having obtained Board of Trade approval, was not able to start public service for another two weeks so that Leeds has the distinction of being the first operator of trolley buses in Great Britain.

The two Leeds vehicles, quickly joined by two more, were similar to the single deck petrol buses then being built, also being painted in the standard tram livery. They had solid tyres and one can only surmise what sort of ride they gave on the roads of the period. So far as the tramways department was concerned the trackless cars proved successful in allowing an economic service to run where laying of a tramway would have been too great an expense. Earlier mention has been made that a tramway extension from Guiseley to Otley, Burley and Ilkley, which the tramways department thought would be uneconomic, was being campaigned for. After considerable negotiation trackless operation was agreed upon, the Guiseley–Otley section being opened on 9 September 1915 followed by the Guiseley–Burley section on 22 October. To operate these additional services four additional trackless vehicles were built, three during the year ending 31 March 1915 and the fourth by 1916. Proposals to open a route from Baildon Bridge to Burley and Otley and to extend the Farnley route to Drighlington, Gildersome and Ardsley were not implemented.

The tramway extensions of 1908–12, and those anticipated for the immediate future required more new cars, to provide which the Corporation implemented a major change of policy by building complete cars themselves at Kirkstall Road works. After 1906 a modified top cover had been designed for fitting to open top cars having full platform canopies, differing from the former type in having fan light ventilation and rather narrower panelling below the windows. This re-designed top cover was used for the new cars, above a longer new style four window body with standard stairs. Brill trucks and Dick Kerr DB1 series controllers were used and contemporary press reports referred to the pleasing internal wood finishes, commenting with satisfaction that the 'ridge' behind the seats had been removed. The first car was numbered 115 and one of its first duties in June 1908 was the official first car to Pudsey when it was driven by the Lady Mayoress. No. 116 soon followed, but the remaining ten, Nos. 117–126 were not built until 1909. Nos. 119 and 120 were used as ceremonial cars at the opening of the Yeadon route.

Improvement of the older cars continued, the new style top deck covers being fitted to the remaining Dick Kerr cars, except for No. 231 which had been illuminated for the Coronation of Kind Edward VII in 1902. This car was used for various similar purposes and was not provided with a top cover until 1921. A design of top cover for non-canopied cars was prepared, having a short roofed but otherwise open section outside the bulkhead which had a central door into the saloon. A short longitudinal seat was provided above the platform steps and fan light ventilation was incorporated. A modified version was soon introduced in which the open area was enclosed, making the whole of the top deck seating area within a saloon but leaving the stairs and platforms exposed. A number of the original type were subsequently modified to the later design. The only major re-construction was of the Greenwood and Batley cars most of which were re-built with platform canopies and full canopy top covers.

Top covered cars were not permitted on Whitecote Hill on the Rodley route – the steepest on the system – and the need to retain open-top cars for this service, thus providing inferior facilities, prompted the Department's Assistant Engineer, A. W. Maley, to devise a track brake which could be operated mechanically as well as electro-magnetically. Dick Kerr car No. 270 was equipped with this in 1907, a demonstration taking place on Whitecote Hill on 26 November when the car was run up to twenty-seven miles per hour, and then stopped in 66 yards. A press photograph of the occasion showed men running beside the car, the caption stating they were carrying tape measures to ascertain the distance in which the car was stopped. The difficulties of this hill were such that a sandman was continuously employed and when the route opened it was also announced that only the most experienced drivers would be allowed to drive on it. Adoption of the track brake permitted top covered cars to be used with safety on this hill, subsequently only cars with mechanical track brakes being allowed to work on any of the 'steep' hills – i.e. Beeston, Rodley and Morley. Certain later designs incorporated such brakes for this purpose, developed to their ultimate potential including air operation by Maley for the EMB Company and later his own firm of Maley and Taunton.

As all routes could now be operated with top covered cars, provision of top-covers was pushed forward, about eighty cars being dealt with during 1906–7, thirty-seven during the years 1907–10, none during 1911, and the remaining fifty-two (except for No. 231) during the year ended 31 March 1913.

During this time the problem of drivers being exposed to the elements and the dust was attracting attention, a press cutting in June 1906 remarking that the previous day had been very troublesome even for pedestrians and that some tram drivers had been wearing motorist's goggles which they had purchased themselves. The writer hoped that the Tramways Management would give consideration to the provision of some protection for the drivers. It was 1909 before anything positive was done and this, of course, was the experimental fitting of platform vestibules to three cars. By March 1912 a further six had been equipped, whilst a new batch of cars had been started at Kirkstall Road works in 1911. These were very similar to Nos. 115–126 but were built with platform vestibules, had more rounded ends and once again reversed stairs. The bodies were a little shorter, seating capacity in the lower saloon being 22 instead of 24 and in the upper 36 instead of 38, the total being 58 instead of 62. The ten cars in this batch were completed by June 1912 and, since all the numbers from 1 to 282 were now occupied, the series was extended by allocating the new cars Nos. 283–292. In a press report on 28 February 1914 No. 289 was featured as a 'standard' tram, described as 'ideal for Leeds'.

The new platform vestibules, or screens as they were called at the time, came in for their first significant test on 13 January 1912 when there was a severe snow storm. The twelve vestibuled cars were working on the Roundhay via Chapeltown service, said to be the most severe for weather on the system and, although the vestibules had not hitherto been popular with drivers because they considered their view would be impaired rather than improved in bad weather, experience on this day caused a change of heart. The Department decided to equip cars with vestibules quickly for use on exposed routes, fitting thirty-three during the remainder of 1912, twenty-six in 1913 and eight in 1914. The old cars vestibuled were mainly of the 1902/4 Brush, Greenwood and Batley, and L.C.T. 1908/9 series.

A further batch of forty-seven new cars was constructed between July 1913 and April 1915, carrying numbers 293–339, in which further minor modifications were introduced which altered the appearance noticeably. The design of vestibule was changed, distinctly flatter ends were introduced and the top deck side panelling was deepened. Construction was stopped after No. 339 because of war conditions, although thirty-three further cars had been authorised and would have been built by Messrs Hurst Nelson had they not had a serious fire.

An accident during 1911 was ascribed to the lack of any side lifeguards, although all Leeds cars were fitted with Tidswell's lifeguards during the early 1900s, Leeds having been the first operator to adopt them. A device was therefore invented to close the gap 'between the trigger and tray' and fitted quickly to all cars, including all subsequent new ones up to 369. This consisted of a metal rod fixed to the front lifeguards being able to run along a second bar fixed between the front bumper and the wooden back support of the lifeguard proper.

The building of these extra cars had created two problems at Kirkstall Road works, the first being that the space required for repairs and maintenance became greater, the second that the space required for traffic cars also became greater. To overcome these problems an extension was made to the Sovereign Street depot during 1912 to accommodate fifty-five cars, so that the equivalent space at Kirkstall Road could be made available for maintenance. A new car shed was then built at Swinegate, being completed in July 1914, but before it could be brought into use, it was requisitioned by the War Department for use as a recruiting office. When this need relaxed it was opened as a depot, only

**Plate 15** 1899 Brush car No. 85 with the first style of short top cover having open ends. Compare windows with car no. 166 on page 28 photographed at Victoria Road about 1912

*(Copyright Leeds City Transport)*

**Plate 16** 1897 Milnes trailer car No. 101, rebuilt as a motor car in 1900 and finally modified with a second style short cover, fully enclosed. Photographed at Victoria Road 1912

*(Copyright Leeds City Transport)*

to be re-requisitioned for use as a clothing store for the remainder of the war. The staff were also moved in December 1915 from offices in Infirmary Street, where the lease had expired, to the well known building in Swinegate, the Yorkshire Rider Bus Company Head Office since October 1986.

An interesting item in the press in June 1921 referred to the hope expressed fifty years before, when construction of the first line to Headingley was just beginning, that railway wagons would be worked along the Kirkstall Road route to various works and factories. This did not materialise, but in 1910/11 the Waterworks Department was building the filter beds at Headingley and reached agreement with the Transport Department for the sand and gravel to be conveyed by tram from a wharf on the River Aire. The Transport Committee's report for the year recorded that suitable wagons with hoppers had been obtained, 28,000 tons of material conveyed, and the financial results were quite satisfactory. These cars had open platforms having a small dash panel and two large tipping hoppers, pivoted to tip over either side, to either side of a central trolley post. After completion of the filter beds their use was extended to the movement of stones and clay from a site on the Wortley route where they became known as commercial cars. One so engaged was involved in an accident on 13 June 1916 when it ran out of control, caught up and collided heavily with the preceding passenger car from Wortley which became derailed, crashing into a wall. In later years these cars were used for permanent way department work and No. 4 (they had a separate series of numbers) remained in Torre Road depot yard, stripped of its hoppers, in 1948.

Many municipal transport undertakings carried parcels on quite a large scale but Leeds had never been keen to do this. A report of 5 December 1904 quoted the General Manager as saying he was not hurrying to regularise things, that he considered trams were for passengers and doubted the wisdom of inconveniencing them for a doubtful profit. A small business, was, however, carried on and in July 1907 it was reported that the Department had written to forty-eight other undertakings to ascertain their views. The majority of the large municipal ones did not recommend the carrying of parcels, although a number were running successful schemes. However, during 1918 the Ministry of Food asked the Department to augment the service considerably, arrangements being made with twenty-seven shop-keepers to accept and take delivery of parcels. Some premises were taken near the Swinegate Headquarters Offices for a central depot, one special car being used, as well as the front platforms of service cars. Quite a volume of traffic began to flow immediately. The 1919 annual report referred to the expansion of the parcels service having necessitated the depot's being moved to Kings Mill in Sovereign Street and three Ford Motor parcels vans being purchased. In 1921 two additional

Siddeley Deasy parcels vans were obtained and a 21 per cent increase in carryings, to 222,000, was recorded. An increase was recorded nearly every year until 1938 when 541,642 parcels were conveyed. The service was suspended during the second war and was not resumed thereafter, although for many years bundles of newspapers, carried on cars front platforms, were put off at selected newsagents shops, usually accompanied by much sounding of the warning bell by the driver!

The first World War had its effect, all services suffering through the conscription of men, which resulted in staff shortages, although 400 women were soon employed as conductresses, and it was confidently expected that no men would be employed on this work. Shortage of men and materials caused a severe backlog of tramcar repairs to build up and, as stated previously, new construction ceased except for some new hopper cars while track repairs also fell seriously behind. By the end of the war, a number of cars were stored 'unserviceable'.

On top of this running down of equipment, the system suffered other strains, as evidenced by the fact that although car miles remained steady during the years 1915–1919 the passengers carried rose from 95 to 120 million. The General Manager, Mr. Hamilton, had been released for Government service, in organisation of the Shipyard Labour Department, and on his recommendation Messrs. H. G. Jeken and R. B. Holt of the Tramways Department, together with the Gas Department Manager also took up 'responsible duties' under him.

It is common to think that traffic congestion is a modern problem associated with motor cars in our cities but in 1912 the situation round the Corn Exchange was so bad that a new tramway layout was put down in an attempt to keep traffic fluid. The rearrangement included an alteration to the entrance to the gentlemen's toilet at the corner of Vicar Lane and Duncan Street, which at that time formed a large island in the middle of the road. The new layout included the well known loops round the circular loading island and via Kirkgate which eliminated certain crossing movements at the Duncan Street junction, as well as introduction of the third line in Vicar Lane. Cars then loaded at the kerbside in this area, rather than in the centre of the road, while at the same time queue barriers were installed to regulate loading. This operated from 24 June 1912 and an interesting press comment, commending the new arrangements reads:

> The introduction of the queue system should put an end to the unseemly rushes for cars which have taken place at these points at busy periods.

All this development and improvement in the years leading up to the 1914 war, together with the very satisfactory financial situation of the undertaking, gave every indication that the trams would enjoy continuing prosperity and expansion. They seemed to be the answer to the

**Plate 17** Hamilton 1910 balcony car No. 289, when new in April 1912 at Kirkstall Abbey, compare the livery with restored 309 below

*(Copyright Leeds City Transport)*

**Plate 18** 1912 Hamilton balcony car No. 328 after its restoration as No. 309 in 1912 livery. Photographed outside Kirkstall Road works 1948. Compare body with car no. 289 above

*(Copyright Leeds City Transport)*

transport problem. But although in many respects this was the case the first seeds for their downfall had already been sown. The housing situation previously described – concentrated areas of back-to-back building – was already being seen by many people to be very undesirable. The older property, especially that dating from before about 1868, was particularly bad, because until that time there had been virtually no control over builders concerning the numbers of houses which could be put on a given area of land, the provision of damp courses, sanitation or water supplies, the latter often being shared. Slum clearance began as early as 1870 with a policy of limited demolition to open up the congested areas between houses and courts, while by 1878 a larger scheme had been undertaken involving an acre in the Union Street area, on which 222 houses were demolished at a cost of £24,940. Part of the cleared area was used for new streets, swimming baths, a police station and an extension to the markets. A further scheme in 1894 involved one and a half acres in the East Street area which were cleared at a cost of £11,127 involving 104 dwellings and two public houses. After the clearance streets were laid out and the land sold as building plots, this scheme being followed in 1895 by one for the Quarry Hill area. It had originally been intended to redevelop a small area but it soon became evident that this would achieve nothing worthwhile and a comprehensive scheme was the only solution. An area of 66¾ acres was tackled, new wide roads being planned through the area – the former New York Road and existing Regent Street and St. Peter's Street – and after Parliamentary approval in 1901 all the property was purchased for ultimate demolition. The last houses were not demolished until 1933 but the early start and planning enabled the rebuilding to be undertaken when the time was opportune.

The city was expanding throughout this period, most of the building being of through terrace or back-to-back houses and although building of the latter was prohibited by Parliament in 1909, Leeds sought and obtained permission to build those already authorised so that the last ones were not completed until the 1930s. The Corporation's argument was that such houses were better for people who lived in them than the tenement blocks which would have been the alternative. New building, however, was declining throughout the first decade of the new century, by 1907 it was less than 1,000 per annum, while in 1913–14 it was only 300. This building was taking place in new areas which were beyond reasonable walking distance from the city and there followed extensions to a number of routes which indicate clearly where the building took place:

| | |
|---|---|
| Headingley – West Park | 11 Sept. 1908 |
| West Park – Lawnswood | 18 April 1913 |
| Killingbeck – Halton | 30 April 1915 |

| | |
|---|---|
| Killingbeck – Killingbeck Cemetery | 20 May 1916 |
| Cross Flatts Park – Dewsbury Road Terminus | 14 Aug 1915 |

In addition, in writing the 1911 Leeds City Tramways Guide, the well known Leeds historian Alfred Mattison recorded that the evidence of the builders work extended on the Roundhay Road route from Artillery Terrace to Harehills Lane. This housing was all of the older type, although beyond Spencer Place including through as well as the back-to-back type, the population on this route thus becoming particularly dense. Demolition of the older back-to-back houses has largely been completed in this area, so the wheel has turned full circle! Redevelopment so far is of light industry between Sheepscar and the junction with Roseville Road.

During the war no building took place and, by about 1919, the position had deteriorated very seriously. Various housing acts passed after the war gave a great impetus to municipalities to tackle these slum clearance problems and Leeds acquired land at Middleton, Hawksworth Wood, Crossgates, Wyther House and Meanwood for municipal building. Twenty-one local architects were employed, the first house being completed on 8 May 1920 on the Wyther Estate, 3,329 new houses actually being built on all the sites mentioned above at a cost of £3,249,140. The Middleton site was well removed from any existing tram route and a press report of 4 March 1920 referred to applications for houses there 'not being heavy', because access was difficult until the tramway was opened.

This change in standards of housing, the change in choice of area for extensive building and the regulations imposed on builders created a rapid spread of the urban area, which was accompanied by a significant raising of the standards many people were prepared to accept. This is illustrated by a report in the press in March 1920 in which an agent was reported as saying that back-to-back houses were available for £200, Parlour houses for £300, while the corporation houses being built offered equivalent accommodation, including roads and services, at a building cost of £800. Such houses were available at reasonable rentals with the consequence that 'from £600 down it is increasingly difficult to sell for the owners occupation and there is no demand at all for property below £300 in value'.

As the new building areas were much further from the city centre than the old, as each house occupied much more land, and as these changes were accompanied by demolition work in the older most congested areas, the net result was a thinning out of population densities along the main routes. This was perhaps the first major influence to be exerted against the trams, for, although extensions or new routes to serve the new areas were built for many years, these did not enjoy the prosperity of the older routes. The extra distance increased the journey time, which in its turn reduced the proportion of mileage over which a full load was carried, thereby changing unfavourably the ratio between car miles and passenger miles. The greater spread of the new housing estates meant many people had further to walk from the nearest tram stop than had previously been the case, which was not too important a matter in 1920, but which became a very important consideration indeed after 1930. Pressure grew to project routes into the heart of the new development areas but, as had been the case with the projected routes along East Street, Whitehall Road and beyond Guiseley, in many cases such extensions could not be justified for tramway operation. Buses were therefore provided, many of the routes duplicating a trunk tramcar service. It was (and still is) no problem to provide a bus service to two or three termini in a large housing area at a low but satisfactory frequency for both operator and passenger at the extremities and, where the route was common, a high frequency on the trunk route. With tramcar operation this was rare because construction of the low density sections could never be justified.

In 1920, however, the ultimate consequences of the new housing developments were not visualised, the 'bus was not sufficiently developed to serve as anything more than a feeder to the tram route in certain cases, so there remained scope for much tramway development over the next thirty years.

CHAPTER 4

# Enclosed cars in quantity – express tracks

The end of the war in 1918 found the Tramways Department in none too happy a position. The staff shortages in all its departments had allowed arrears of maintenance to reach significant proportions and although a start was made on building new cars in 1919, the pace was very slow compared with the period 1913–15 because of these staff difficulties and raw material shortages, together with the increasing problem of keeping the pre-1906 cars in good running order. The annual report for 1922/3 referred to the rolling stock in general being in good condition, despite the average time in service, such a situation having only been achieved by three years work to overcome the effects of the wartime difficulties, at the expense of new construction.

The track had suffered equally and, after the war, efforts to overcome the arrears of maintenance were severely hampered by a national shortage of cement so that it was not until 1921 that an effective effort could be made in this area. £138,000, well over twice the normal pre-war figure, was spent in that year, causing a deficit of £43,000, the first ever recorded by the Department, on the years operations. The state of the undertaking was the cause of much comment concerning finances and services and many letters were published in the Press. One such report of 20 July 1920 referred to a daily loss of £200, despite fare increases from 10 June 1918 and 3 June 1920. These increases had failed to keep pace with rising costs, wage increases and reductions in hours, the 1919 annual report including a comment that the latter two had jointly caused an increase on the wages bill of 48.7 per cent. The return of men from war service to the works and for platform duties had allowed thirty extra cars per day to be put on the road and, although this yielded a thirteen per cent increase in passengers carried, it was quite inadequate to balance the accounts. The receipts per car mile rose from 10.936 pence in 1915 to 24.695 pence in 1922 but working expenses per car mile for the same period rose from 5.749 pence per mile (little more than the 1894 Roundhay line figure) to 18.070 pence, so that the ratio between receipts and expenses showed a very unhealthy trend. The statutory fare of one penny for one mile still remained in force and powers were sought to alter it to permit a charge of up to twopence per mile for all classes of travel. A press report of August 1921 stated that this had been granted but no fare increase followed.

After 1920 the national economy was going through a very tough period which was evidenced in 1922 by a fall in the number of passengers and hence in receipts. The factors behind this are a historical study in themselves, not unrelated to the mood of those returning from active service and expecting to find marked improvements in living conditions. The great industrial activity of a nation fighting a war had raised wages and standards of comfort but the one feature which was obviously not sharing in this improvement was housing, despite the Government subsidies made available. Leeds, however, did take advantage of this particular situation as described at the end of the previous chapter. The whole balance of international trade and currency exchange had been disrupted by the war, so that a falling of prices resulted, which in 1922 enabled the Transport Department to impose, not without dissension from the staff, a reduction of wages so achieving a saving in direct costs of £23,000 per annum. The general reduction in prices also provided for reductions in expenditure on car repairs and track maintenance with the result that costs began to fall. At the same time, the number of passengers carried again began to increase, so that the improvement in the financial position made it possible to reduce fares, from 1 March 1923 to those existing after the 1918 increase. From then there was a continual improvement in the number of passengers carried, the car miles run and the gross receipts, resulting in a further fare decrease from 1 October 1925. The receipts fell to 15.671 pence per mile but working expenses fell to 11.621 pence per mile leaving a satisfactory balance. A considerable proportion of this was transferred to the Corporation for general use, thus offsetting the rates, the cumulative total so transferred reaching £1,902,282 in 1930. Tramway operation was apparently still able to continue on a satisfactory financial base.

Before the wage and price reductions took full effect the General Manager, Mr. Hamilton, was talking about the daily deficit, his views on 'unequal competition' and the burden upon his Department of road maintenance costs being quoted on 29 September 1921. Tramway undertakings were required by law to maintain the road surface 'over the four rails and for eighteen inches either side' which was always a sore point with Managers who claimed they did not use the road at all. Those responsible for Tramway permanent way naturally sought to keep costs down when relaying or track repairing was necessary, often using stone setts on either side of the rail to ease the task of uncovering the rails. This in later years provided a poor surface, with dangerous conditions often existing where rails had become badly worn or joints had sunk. In Leeds the area of tramway department maintenance was invariably hand laid, contrasting very poorly after 1945 with the machine laid portion at the sides. The interesting point is that as soon as the financial position deteriorated the iniquity of this situation was brought forward.

The tramway operators' liabilities in this respect could not be escaped by withdrawing the service, as subsequent removal of the track and re-instatement of the road remained their responsibility. This first occurred in Leeds in 1922 when, on 15 June, the short Whitehall Road tram service was discontinued. Its retention for so long after the trolley buses started in June 1911 seems surprising, for the trams were only short workings along the trolley bus route, on that part having the least residential development. Removal of the track and re-instatement of the road was carried out at once, at a cost of £5,490. The arguments about the question of Tramway Department costs in this connection were a major feature in any debates on their retention or otherwise. The need to restore the road surface after maintenance or removal was not disputed, only the requirement for maintenance of the road.

The comments in letters to the press after the war made it clear that the existing tramway system was not held in high regard by many of those who had to make use of it and the management realised that improvements to track and cars were essential. As described at the end of the previous chapter the new residential areas were a much greater distance from the centre and, as the annual cost of track and road maintenance was very high, – £80,000 to £90,000 even after the special effort of 1921 – the reduced cost of construction and maintenance of tracks separate from the road demonstrated in Liverpool and Birmingham showed the desirability of this type of track. The decision was taken to adopt separate tracks wherever practicable and powers were obtained to permit the transfer of tram tracks, during any road improvements or widenings, to other positions including separate tracks where practicable. These separate tracks, generally referred to as 'reserved' tracks in recent years were known as 'express' tracks in Leeds, generally and officially.

The route to serve the new Corporation Estate at Middleton was planned on this basis, but the degree of separation from the road was far greater than usual, the route leaving the road entirely and travelling through Middleton Woods. The original idea was to start the private right of way from Jack Lane but the costs and difficulties of bridging the four-track LMSR Leeds–Sheffield line led to a revised scheme to leave Dewsbury Road via Moor Road with normal street tramway and begin the express section across Hunslet Moor alongside the very old Middleton Railway, at that time operated by the Middleton Estates Company, after which the line curved away into the woods beyond the

**Plate 19** Single deck trolley bus No. 501 at New Farnley

*(Copyright Leeds City Transport)*

**Plate 20** Double deck trolley buses Nos 510, 511, 512 lined up outside Kirkstall Road works

*(Copyright Leeds City Transport)*

over-bridge carrying the former Great Northern Railway line from Hunslet East Goods station to Beeston Junction. The land, like that for the housing estate itself, was purchased from the Middleton Estates Company and construction of the formation started in November 1920. This was used from 1921–4 for a contractors railway to convey the vast amount of raw material required for the new Estate during which period the new residents on the Estate had to make do with a bus service to Dewsbury Road. In 1923 sufficient building progress had been made to justify starting construction of the tramway and in 1924 powers were obtained for the section in Moor Road and across Hunslet Moor. Work was thereafter pushed ahead with great rapidity.

In the meantime it had been decided to put the Roundhay line on a separate alignment between Harehills and Roundhay Park except for a short length between the two parades of shops at Oakwood which remained in the centre of the road, because space precluded the extra land being obtained. This too was pressed forward quickly, the new alignment being brought into use in two stages, the first from Harehills to Oakwood on 21 May 1922 and the second from Oakwood to Roundhay Park on 23 July 1923. On these first sections the rails were laid on wooden sleepers and covered with ballast so that only the rail top showed above. Five inch rails were used at first but they were replaced by seven inch ones together with an increased depth of ballast on the Roundhay sections in 1929 and on the down grade in Middleton Woods in 1930. The aim of these tracks was two-fold, to reduce construction and maintenance costs by avoiding associated road works, and to permit faster 'express' running by separation from other road traffic and fencing off from pedestrians. The Roundhay stretches were at the side of the road with central 'T' bracket poles to support the overhead. There were unfortunate conflictions with other traffic at each of the four entrances/exits because of the side position, that at the Easterly Road junction becoming very difficult in later years after the roundabout was made as the tram tracks were not moved and passed through the middle of it. The present arrangements, introduced in 1972 controlled by traffic lights, would have accommodated the trams with great advantage!

The Middleton route also had centre poles and the extension in 1927 ran at the side of the road, but without crossing it. All the remaining stretches were in the central area of a dual carriageway with side support poles and span wires. The centre poles were never changed, however, and remained until the routes concerned closed, after which they were removed because, unlike the side poles, they could not be used for street lighting purposes.

The Leeds Corporation Act of 1925 authorised such tracks to be built in York Road, Stanningley Road and Otley Road, although immediate implementation was not possible. The fullest use was made of the powers, all new lines being laid in this way wherever possible, the only exceptions after 1920 proving to be Moor Road on the Middleton route, the very short extension at Dewsbury Road and the well-known bottleneck past Killingbeck Hospital on the Crossgates route which was particularly bad as the trams came from a central reservation to the very kerb edge, leaving no space at all for other vehicles. The 1949 extension from Belle Isle to Middleton was partly away from the road and partly at the side, to meet up with the 1927 line, but with side poles and span wires.

The continuing growth of the urban area by council and private building justified extensions, the Middleton line already described being brought into use on 12 November 1925 with an extension from Middleton Park Avenue along the roadside to Lingwell Road on 26 November 1927. Cross Gates was an area which was extensively developed about this time and an extension from Killingbeck Cemetery to Cross Gates was opened on 23 September 1924.

Another interesting route opened in 1924 was that to Templenewsam, which was really an extension of the Halton line, especially so after 1936 when Halton cars used a crossover and the original line was abandoned. Templenewsam House, where Lord Darnley, first husband of Mary, Queen of Scots, was born in 1545, was owned latterly by Lord Halifax, but in 1922 he sold it to the Corporation for £35,000. One of the reasons for this decision was reputed to be the smell from Knostrop Sewage Works which can be very noticeable with the wind in the right (or wrong) direction, but whatever the reasons the city acquired a magnificent park and a notable house at a bargain price. It should be recalled that the area purchased was 935 acres compared with 616 acres at Roundhay costing £139,000 fifty years earlier and that Kirkstall Abbey was purchased for £10,000. Access to Templenewsam was difficult, and in order to develop it as a park, it was decided to build the tram route. The road from Halton was used only for access to intermediate points and as dual carriageway was quite unjustified a side reservation was built, the last stretch to the terminus being away from the road, which was for that part only used by pedestrians to reach the house. Except at summer weekends and holidays the service was half-hourly and generally operated from Kirkgate only. The route was opened in two stages on 18 and 21 April 1924 and continued in operation until the final closure on 7 November 1959. Some considerable expenditure was then necessary on improvement of the road to permit operation of the replacement bus service.

The first really serious accident occurred during this period on Saturday 12 May 1923, when car No. 191 working the 07.00 from Churwell became out of control, ran away down the 1 in 11 Churwell bank, left the rails and turned over. Seven passengers were killed and thirty-five injured and an official Board of Trade Enquiry was held by Lt. Col. A. H. Mount. The car was equipped with the standard hand wheel brake for normal service use, electric emergency brake and mechanical track brake for use on hilly routes and, when it was examined after the accident, the hand brake was found to be partially defective. Immediately after the incident the driver was discovered wandering in the road in a dazed state and was not able to say clearly how he left the front platform. Two of the passengers killed had remained on the front platform attempting to stop the car. These men were posthumously commended for their gallantry but, although the high speed by then attained would have considerably complicated matters and Lt. Col. Mount considered that the car's other brakes should have enabled it to be kept under control, it seems probable that lack of knowledge frustrated their efforts. Lt. Col. Mount attributed the accident to the driver's losing his nerve at a critical time, when he found the hand-brake was not operating correctly, and failing to make proper use of the other brakes available to keep the car under control.

Construction of new cars had begun again in 1919 with car No. 340, a continuation of the order begun in 1913 with No. 293 and delayed by the war after No. 339 was completed in 1915. As mentioned before progress was slow, further delay being caused waiting for trucks to be delivered in 1920, so that only eleven cars were placed in service between October 1919 and August 1921. No design changes were incorporated except that the Peckham pendulum P.22 truck was introduced as a standard with cars 346/7/9/50, whilst some had 7′6″ wheelbase rather than 6′6″ wheelbase Hurst Nelsons. There was some improvement in production after that and the order was completed with Nos. 368/9 on 30 June 1923, most of the last fifteen also having P.22 trucks.

The design, however, was basically unaltered from the 1908 Leeds built cars, except for the addition of platform vestibules and a superior truck, and it was realised that something better was needed. Before the standard order was finished a totally enclosed car numbered 370 was built at Kirkstall Road Works and placed in service at the end of May 1923. A press report of 25 May 1923 concerning the appearance of this vehicle stated it was operating on the Roundhay–Kirkstall section and suggested people should keep an eye open for this new venture into luxury travel. This was high praise indeed for the only real advance was the enclosing of the ends of the top deck, wooden seats being retained throughout with the old-fashioned longitudinal seats in the lower saloon. Reversed stairs were also retained but the car had a 17′6″ long body and the seating capacity was raised to an unprecedented (for Leeds) seventy. Some preliminary work on this design had been done and at least one of the latter balcony cars had the top deck end panelling secured to the canopy top in the manner of the enclosed cars and of the same depth as the sides. Cars 371–5, similar to No. 370, were placed in service between January and March 1924, but No. 376 completed in April had normal halfturn stairs. All these had wooden vestibules at the top of the stairs with a door. The body used on No. 376 proved to be the final 'Hamilton' standard and between June 1924 and May 1925 a further sixteen, Nos. 377–92 were built with P.22 trucks, although No. 389 had a 7′6″ wheelbase P.35 truck and No. 392 a Craven truck which was very similar in appearance to the standard P.22. Three bar lifeguards were introduced with No. 370, and at the same time the single metal side guard was replaced by three wooden slats. None of the earlier Hamilton cars were altered to conform, however, except No. 321 when that was rebuilt in 1938.

Three further similar cars numbered 393–5 were built in August, September and October 1925 and with these the EMB 'Pivotal' truck was introduced into Leeds. This was one of many attempts to create riding characteristics in a four wheel car comparable with those of a bogie car, but having the benefits of two motors rather than four and their attendant costs. The Pivotal truck was in essence a two wheel bogie, giving a wheel base of 10 feet, very long for a four wheel car. To permit satisfactory negotiation of corners the two parts of the truck were allowed a degree of movement by being connected to the car through rollers and to each other by a system of cross-linking levers. The theory that a single pair of wheels would pivot the truck the correct way on a corner and then restore it to straight did not prove sound in everyday practice and there were considerable difficulties. These were eventually overcome by eliminating the rollers and locking the cross-linkage. Two hundred truck sets were ordered straight away but once the locking up had taken place they became very reliable indeed. As late as 1948 car No. 10 came into Kirkstall Road works after running 100,000 repair free miles. The long wheelbase obviated much of the see-saw motion experienced with Brill, Hurst Nelson and P.22 trucks of 6′6″ or 7′6″ wheelbase, but in later years, especially during the 1939–45 war period, they became very run down. In that condition they rode over bad joints very heavily and achieved an alarming degree of side to side oscillation which normal repairing did little to mitigate. One or two cars still running on them in 1951/2 (I remember No. 117 in particular) had them thoroughly overhauled so that interested observers were able to obtain an idea of what they had been like in their hey-day, when the ride must have compared very favourably with the older types of four-wheel truck, also with many designs of bogie.

A new and not too successful innovation with cars 394/5 was air brake equipment, but the problems were with the Pivotal trucks and air brakes were successfully fitted, from 1926, to all the 45 cars (both enclosed and open balconied) mounted on P.22 trucks. This comprised either EMB or, later, Maley and Taunton air track brake equipment together with Maley mechanical and electro-magnetic track brakes. The air valve was added to the controller – either DB1 K3 or K4 – the handle being altered to operate with an off position at right angles to the driver,

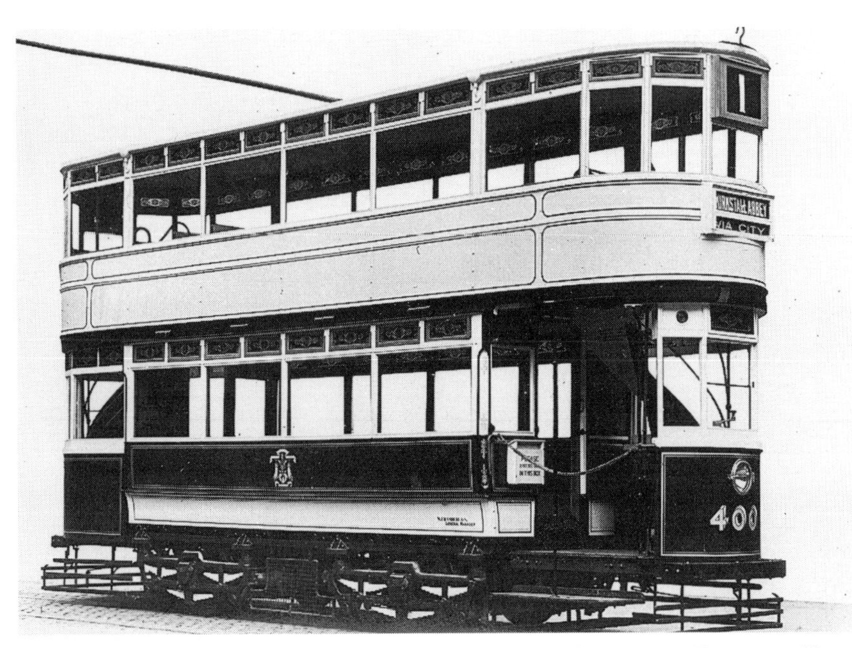


**Plate 21** The prototype Chamberlain car No. 400 when new in Dec 1925. Note the indicator positions, the new blue livery and first style pivotal trucks

*(Copyright Leeds City Transport)*

**Plate 22** Hamilton enclosed car No. 380, in royal blue livery at Corn Exchange 19 April 1950

*(Author)*

the admission valve being one notch towards the driver from 'off' and release half a notch forward. The air track then became the service brake, assisted by the hand wheel brake, with the mechanical track brake available for steep hills and the magnetic track for emergency braking. Latterly these cars predominated on the Beeston route gaining the soubriquet 'Beeston Air Brake'. The workings took them as much to Harehills, Meanwood and Elland Road, but the Beeston association remained. These were the only cars to operate in Leeds which officially relied entirely on a track brake of any sort for service braking.

During 1925 specifications were being pushed forward for the two hundred new cars which were mounted on the EMB Pivotal trucks, of which only fifty were to be built by the Department. Before this was finalised Mr. Hamilton died, having been General Manager since 1902. He was responsible for the major development of the system and held a unique position in the city from 1913 when, as a result of his efforts during the Municipal strike, he had been appointed Commercial Manager, for which he received a separate salary. He was succeeded by Mr. (later Sir William) Chamberlain from Oldham and it was after him that most of the two hundred new cars became known. The obvious similarity between the Oldham cars he built, the 1926–7 Leeds cars and the 1930 Belfast cars, to which City he transferred in 1928, however, makes it plain that his influence was strongly exerted upon the designs.

The new cars from Kirkstall started to appear in December 1925 in a rather haphazard way, No. 400, prototype for the new design, and No. 396 with a standard 'Hamilton' body, being placed in service on 12 December. The main innovations in the new car were in the body, the stair-head vestibules being replaced by folding trap doors, which drivers invariably put up and down very noisily, the length being increased to 18 feet and the seating capacity being further raised to 72. Fan light ventilation was retained, but two separately opening windows were provided above each full window, the lines of the car being smoothed out round the front top deck and in particular the vestibules, while red stained glass was used in the fan lights. A major innovation with this car was the provision of a large roller-blind route number display box in the top of the front top deck window. Route numbers had been allocated to services for many years but never displayed and on the new car an additional space was provided for a route blind in addition to the destination blind, these two occupying part of the space used for the end advertisements which this car rarely carried. No further cars were built like this, but 400 was never altered, running until 4 October 1951. It also incorporated a minor alteration to the side lifeguards, the metal rod being dispensed with and the side guards being hung independently. However, wooden seating remained as did the Pivotal truck and the car relied on the hand wheel brake for service use.

A more striking change was the introduction of a new blue livery – Mr.

Chamberlain made the same change in Belfast – which comprised blue dash and lower deck side panels with cream rocker and top deck side panels and window frames. All the new cars were painted in this style as well as many older ones which remained in service. However, some chocolate, primrose and white re-painting of pre-1906 cars took place after 1926.

Although the first 'Chamberlain' style car had been produced at Kirkstall Road, further standard 'Hamilton' cars numbered 397–405 continued to be built up to October 1926 of which 399 and 401/2 had P.22 trucks and the rest EMB Pivotal with some variations in electrical equipment using types which became standard in the new cars. Full details are in Appendix B. Starting with No. 390 roof rainwater guttering was introduced and became standard from No. 396 whilst the new style three blind indicator was standardised from No. 404. The contracts for the other 150 new cars were let to the Brush Electrical Engineering Company and to English Electric for seventy-five cars each while Kirkstall Road built thirty-five similar to No. 400, but with the full indicator mounted in the front upper saloon window, as had all the contract built cars. All these cars had EMB Pivotal trucks, the contract built ones being delivered to a temporary depot at the Airedale Foundry for placing on the trucks, and, except for forty of the Brush ones, Metro-Vick electrical equipment. Fifty of the Pivotal trucks used on cars fitted with Metro-Vick equipment were fitted with Hoffmann roller bearings, which had been experimented with on No. 396. There were noticeable body differences in the three versions, especially in the setting of the vestibule windows, both above, and below and round the ends of the top deck, including the destination blind boxes. Internally the destination boxes were noticeably different, the English Electric cars having a single door for access to the route number blind whilst the others had two. There was no move towards upholstered seats or air brakes with these cars although Nos. 24 and 39 were equipped with the latter. Unlike Nos. 394/5, which soon lost their equipment, these two retained it until 1938. All the real Chamberlain Pivotal cars had hand brake stanchions designed to accommodate the Maley mechanical track brake wheel but only Nos. 24/39 ever had such equipment.

Once delivery got under way, 198 new cars were put on the road between February 1926 and October 1927, the Leeds built cars being the last, having Nos. 411–45, whilst the contract built cars started again from No. 1, 1–75 being the Brush cars and 76–150 the English Electric. This influx made possible the withdrawal of a large number of the pre 1906 cars, now very outdated and, as described earlier, incurring excessive maintenance costs.

A few old cars had already gone, Nos. 133/8/47/8/63/70/7/80 sold to the West Riding Company during the war in 1917 to replace cars destroyed in a depot fire, No. 191 destroyed in the Churwell Hill accident, No. 184

after some front entrance experiments in 1914, the odd single decker No. 49 and one or two withdrawn after 1920. However, in the year ended 31 March 1928 102 of the pre 1906 cars were dismantled. Those that remained, plus Nos. 115–26, acquired an 'A' suffix to the number, if numbered between 1 and 150.

The numbers 406–410 were still unused and new Pivotal trucked cars were built to fill them in 1928. Surprisingly, perhaps, these were an 18 foot version of the standard 'Hamilton', the only obvious difference being the indicator, where the full new blinds were provided in the first place similar to Nos. 404/5 but distinct from the older 'Hamilton's which started with a destination only blind in the middle of the front upper saloon window, and were later modified, some not until 1933. No. 407 came first on 28 January 1928, with standard Metro-Vick equipment, followed by No. 406 on 17 February on which there was a reversion to DB series controllers and the DK 83 B4 motors used on most of the Pivotal cars between 393 and 405. These motors were inordinately noisy, and as these cars also had disc wheels which added a 'ring', they were about the noisiest cars I remember hearing anywhere! The remaining three cars all had Metro-Vick equipment and were in service by August 1928.

The new cars were regarded as successful, a note in the 1927/8 report to the Council stating they were giving every satisfaction, but, Mr. Chamberlain having departed for Belfast, and been replaced by Mr. R. L. Horsfield, moves were made towards the provision of a car incorporating as many new and modern features as possible and the elimination of the remaining pre 1906 cars. The 'modern' car thus made its appearance in Leeds in February 1930 with two prototypes built at Kirkstall Road incorporating a number of new features and differing in electrical equipment. The body incorporated straight sides to the lower saloon, the rocker panels being dispensed with, and transverse seating was introduced in the lower saloon with red leather upholstery throughout both saloons. The lights were recessed and had frosted glass covers, while pneumatic bells from the platform, the upper saloon over the platform entrance and centrally in the lower saloon, provided a marked contrast to the leather cord running through the strap holders on the lower deck operating a mechanical bell on the platform and the need to use a whistle or stamp on the trap door from upstairs on the other cars. Quarter turn stairs were re-introduced together with stair-head vestibule and door instead of the traps. Fan light ventilation was retained in the lower saloon, but in the upper saloon the four main side windows were in separate wooden frames which could be dropped. Curved glass was used for the end corners, while attention was paid externally to obtaining a smooth appearance. The result was a very handsome car, but, in relation to its size, with a limited seating capacity of sixty because single seats were provided in both saloons at one side of the gangway. Their parentage in Horsfield's 'low bridge' cars for Cardiff is apparent if photographs are compared.

Modern equipment was provided, No. 151 having GEC KA.1 controllers and a Smith Pendulum truck, while No. 152 had BTH 525A controllers and a P.35 truck. Both cars had hand (mainly for parking) and air wheel, with air, magnetic and mechanical track brakes, of which the air wheel was the normal service brake being operated by a separate valve to the right of the controller. An emergency stop with one of these cars was very effective indeed! A further new departure was the use of twenty-seven inch wheels and high speed motors – BTH or GEC types, and on the P.35 trucked car Hoffmann roller bearings were used. In July and September 1930 two similar cars were built of which No. 153 had GEC electrical equipment and an EMB Flexible axle truck of the type later extensively used in Dundee, equipped with Skefco roller bearings. Although no other Leeds car was so equipped, No. 153 retained it until withdrawn in March 1959. No. 154 had BTH equipment and a Hoffmann roller bearing P.35 truck. The 1930/1 report gives some description of these very successful prototypes, records that they were inspected by deputations from the West Riding Company, Edinburgh, Dundee, Glasgow, Sunderland and others, that one comment was that 'they were the finest car at present on the road', and that some undertakings were copying the design.

Their success was such that one hundred similar cars were ordered from Brush, half with BTH equipment and Maley and Taunton air brake equipment similar to No. 152, and half with GEC equipment and Peters air brake equipment. The P.35 truck was standardised, with Hoffmann roller bearings for BTH cars and Skefco for GEC cars, although certain BTH cars had Skefco bearings, and in the latter years few retained the Hoffmann type. Delivery was rapid, No. 155 being placed in service on 14 March 1931, while the last ones were Nos. 252/3, 221, 254 and 244 (in that order) placed in service in January 1932. The hundred cars were thus put on the road in ten months. No. 151 was soon 'standardised' with a P.35 Skefco truck and the cars were a very great success, the BTH ones in particular lasting until the very end of operation, and even in the mid 1950s when they had been newly overhauled they were still of a standard comparable with the average bus in comfort and superior in performance. No. 180 operates at the National Tramway Museum at Crich in Derbyshire for those who wish to savour the experience.

This second influx of new cars – which brought the total of new cars built to 307 for the five years 1926–31 – virtually saw the end of the old cars, 104 of them being dismantled in 1931/2 but 21 continued, most with 'A' suffixes until some further new cars and route rationalisations finished them off by 1938.

The other significant feature of this period was the improvement and

**Plate 23** General view of Briggate/Boar Lane crossing about 1933, showing Hamilton balcony No. 298, 1928 style pivotal No. 406, English Electric pivotal No. 136 and two unidentified balconies

*(Copyright Yorkshire Post Newspapers)*

**Plate 24** General view of the evening rush in Briggate on a wet evening about 1936, showing cars 443 (LCT Chamberlain), 80 (English Electric Chamberlain) and a Brush Chamberlain. Note the crowds at 6.25 pm

*(Copyright Yorkshire Post Newspapers)*

development of the motor bus. As described earlier the trackless tram, or trolley-bus, was the first idea developed as an alternative to tramway operation where expected business could not justify the provision of the necessary fixed assets and this proved reasonably satisfactory. Improved trackless vehicles were developed after the war, the double deck vehicle being introduced in 1921. Two additional double deckers were built in 1922, as well as two new single deckers, one of which had front wheel drive. The double deckers were numbered 510/1/2 and were massive looking vehicles, being modified standard tram bodies altered to have a rear platform only and mounted on a railless chassis. It seems probable that the new construction, which caused the size of the trackless fleet to rise from eight in 1920 to fifteen in 1925 was one of the factors which allowed closure of the Whitehall Road tram route. By the middle twenties, however, the design of motor buses had improved very considerably and it was decided to substitute them for the trackless trams. This took place on the Whitehall Road route in 1926, whilst eight trackless vehicles were operating the Guiseley–Burley/Otley routes in 1927/8. These were finally replaced from 26 July 1928. The trolley bus services in Bradford which were inaugurated on the same day in 1911 as those of Leeds carried on until May 1972 to be the last in Britain operated by traditional vehicles. A new generation of trolley buses will start operation in Bradford in 1991 as a national 'experiment'.

Motor bus operation was expanded, the fleet rising from 23 vehicles in 1925 to 94 in 1931, route mileage reaching 86¼ in the year ending 31 March 1930. Their operation was not profitable at this period, costs being 10.411 pence per vehicle mile with receipts at only 9.857 pence per vehicle mile which in the 1929/30 report was attributed to the sparse population in the areas served. It was, however, considered that the routes operated were useful public services and that in time the financial position would improve. This prognosis proved correct in the following year when bus receipts exceeded expenses for the first time.

The last twelve months before Mr. W. Vane Morland took over saw one or two interesting changes, the most important being closure of the Crown Point Road Power station on 31 March 1932. The Department had generated its own power since the first electrification in 1897 (the Roundhay line also having been self supporting in this respect from 1891 to 1896) and during the coal strike the station had been converted to oil burning, reverting to coal afterwards. After the closure power was obtained from the Corporation Electricity Department and after 1948 the Yorkshire Electricity Board. The original agreement was one which was to the advantage of the Transport undertaking by providing quite cheap traction current. The changes in the charging system in the early fifties resulted in Leeds paying rather more which has been given as a reason for the tramcar abandonment policy. In fact the final decision to change over to buses was made before the alteration in electricity charges.

During this time Swinegate depot was enlarged to accommodate 199 cars, which enabled Hunslet shed to be closed and Kirkstall Road to be closed as a running shed and devoted entirely to repair work. A start was made on doubling the Compton Road route, the Nippet Lane portion being doubled after road widening was completed, and a start was also made on automation with fourteen automatic frogs being provided for the overhead. A new departure was the provision of automatic point changing equipment at one site and this was a guide to future developments.

The tenure of J. B. Hamilton had been a long one, whereas that of W. Chamberlain was a short one of three years, and that of his successor R. L. Horsfield was also unhappily cut short after three years in 1931. W. Vane Morland was appointed to give advice and assistance from January 1932 and took up the full duties from 1 April 1932. His proved to be another long tenure, the start of which heralded some significant changes of policy.

**Plate 25** City Square 20 April 1950. Many of the buildings have now been demolished and the central area as been remodelled. Cars 462 (ex Hull 159) 443 (LCT Chamberlain) and 119 (English Electric Chamberlain) are visible

*(Author)*

CHAPTER 5

# Rationalisation and modernisation

The year 1932/3 was one of extremes of pressure for the tramway undertaking. During the summer the Great Yorkshire Show was held at Templenewsam, for which 9,670 additional vehicle miles were run, and the Northern Command Tattoo was held at Roundhay Park, requiring 27,955 additional miles. During the winter there was an exceptionally severe influenza epidemic which at its peak reduced the staff by 500, and then there was the 'Great Blizzard' when snow fell from 3.0 pm Thursday 23 February to 6.0 pm on Sunday 26 February 1933, resulting in a loss of 67,602 vehicle miles. Road access to Middleton was severed and all milk and food was taken out by tram. The following quote from the 1932–3 committee report to the council summarises the effect of these events very succinctly:

> curiously enough the latter incidents were preceded by the heaviest Christmas traffic in the history of the department. The chief characteristics of the year thus present an interesting sidelight on the activities of a great industrial city. They show the cause and effect of extraordinary and sometimes unexpected circumstances affecting the movement and life of its population, together with the exceptionally heavy demands these make on the transport undertaking.

These things apart, the year saw the closure of the first important route, caused by the decision to abandon trams by another company, when tram working to Rothwell over the West Riding company's tracks ceased on 31 May, and this proved a harbinger of events to follow.

As mentioned in the previous chapter the buses were operated at a profit for the first time in 1931–2 and their role had imperceptibly changed from that of feeding the tram routes and providing a necessary public service, to one of serving the areas to which tramway construction had previously seemed unjustifiable. Development of modern housing and the clearance of slums was creating new areas of population, with a density much less than had previously been normal, to which tramway extension was not going to be an economical proposition, and the increasing general road traffic was making operation of trams on the single track sections unsatisfactory. On the other hand the reserved track sections and the new cars were very successful.

It was therefore decided that wholesale scrapping of trams was not justified in Leeds but extension of the system was to be restricted to reserved track routes and the single track sections were to be replaced by buses. The remaining routes were to be developed and modernised.

The period 1931–3 was a very significant one for the future development of the city. The first ten years of municipal house building had been notable, the ten thousandth house being built in November 1933, but the problem in 1931 was described by the Medical Officer of Health as being whether or not 33,000 back-to-back houses of the old type could be improved and made habitable. This was thought to be doubtful and the alternative was complete demolition. A Housing Committee did not exist until November 1933, when one was created with the Rev. Charles Jenkinson as chairman. He had issued a minority report prior to this, when a health committee member, and this formed the basis of what was done by his housing committee after it came into being. The main aim was the demolition of 30,000 houses in six years and during 1933–5 8,011 houses were represented for demolition, whilst contracts were let for 6,866 houses and flats. A new policy, bitterly opposed, involving differential rents was introduced and a major change of principle was the acceptance of the idea of rehousing families and not total numbers of persons as had been previously the case.

Quarry Hill Flats were a product of this phase of housing improvement and were an imposing testimony to the determination to rehouse those families which had sub-standard accommodation. The development area included 938 flats covering twenty-six acres and housing 3,280 people, but only fourteen per cent of the ground area was built on. The remainder was open space. Such a vast single development has not been repeated, although when they were in vogue Tower Blocks became a feature of the city, but Quarry Hill finally became too expensive to maintain, largely because of the innovations in construction inherent in the concept, and was demolished in 1978. Redevelopment of the site has started with the construction and opening in 1990 of the West Yorkshire Playhouse on its permanent site.

Leeds was a city of narrow streets, particularly those running east to west, although Briggate was reasonably wide, wide enough to have queue barriers in the centre of the road which allowed trams to load at the front without obstructing traffic too much. Park Row and Cookridge Street had been improved by the resiting and rebuilding of St. Anne's Cathedral, formerly in the middle of the road, and Vicar Lane had been improved in the early 1900s, the new markets being built on the site of the vicarage, the land for which had been given to the church in 1453.

Only Boar Lane had any semblance of a main east west street. A major improvement was completed in 1933 when the Headrow was opened as a wide dual carriageway, one side of the old Upper and Lower Head Row being demolished and replaced between Vicar Lane and the Town Hall by new buildings of similar architectural pattern. The continuation from there to Westgate and Wellington Bridge was not completed until the early 1950s and has now been overtaken by urban motorway developments whilst the Headrow itself has been closed to through traffic between Briggate and Park Row/Cookridge Street to ensure such traffic uses the motorway.

The housing programme had continued the trend started in the 1920s by thinning out the areas of population along the original trunk sections of the main routes and expanding the urban area. Two large new areas for housing development were selected, at Seacroft and Belle Isle, and plans were prepared for serving those areas by tram routes. There had been a considerable area built along York Road in the Killingbeck area and the first section of one of the suggested Seacroft routes was opened along Gipton Approach on 11 September 1936. This was a central reservation 660 yd long with side poles and span wires, laid in concrete and incorporating a substantial cutting to keep the gradient less than that which would require operation by track brake equipped cars. The route was intended to continue along Wykebeck Valley Road, South Parkway and North Parkway to form a small circular loop at Seacroft. Cars worked through between Gipton Estate and Lower Wortley. The first extension beyond Balm Road terminus towards Belle Isle was authorised in 1935, but was not proceeded with at once.

Modernisation of the sections of the tramway system to be retained started in earnest in 1933, with the first stage in May of a programme for converting the overhead system to 'centre wire' running. This involved the provision of large numbers of additional poles to support span wires instead of the side bracket poles used to support the former 'off centre' wires and to replace the centre poles in Roundhay Road at Harehills but, particularly in the city area, considerable use was made of wall rosettes to eliminate the poles altogether and in the 1933–4 report the transport committee acknowledged the help of the property owners in this way. The forward thinking of the 1891 Sheepscar–Oakwood electrification engineers in using a span wire and side pole system must be noted here. Had this been copied in the Corporation's electrification in 1897–1902 much of this work would have been avoided and the benefits which were realised from 1935 would have been available all the time. The single track routes which were to be taken over by the buses were not at first altered and when the change took place poles were recovered for use on routes being dealt with – those from the Hyde Park routes being reported as recovered in the 1933–4 report although the trams did not stop running until January 1934. At the same time as the overhead was altered, triangular automatic trolley reversers were installed in it at many terminals and automatic points were extensively introduced. These were an electro-magnetic-spring arrangement operated from the overhead, on the basis that with power being drawn from the overhead the points remained or changed to the right and with power not being drawn they remained or changed to the left. These were a great time saver at junctions, most of which were naturally at busy road intersections. They did have their problems, however, as the position ahead of the points at which the overhead wire switch had to be placed, in order to ensure that a second car did not change them underneath the first one, meant that if the points failed to operate properly there was little chance of the driver stopping despite the slow speed approach inherent in their use, even with power applied. The resultant reversing move in busy traffic, particularly if other cars were close behind, caused many hold-ups, and I have recollections of three or four cars having to reverse in order that the one on the wrong route could reverse far enough to allow the driver to use his hand point rod. Great care had to be taken by a driver pushing a failed car and I remember a line of cars stretching the whole length of North Street after No. 21, being pushed after failure, had stopped with the front wheels up New Briggate and the rear ones towards Vicar Lane.

The work on the overhead was completed on 3 December 1938 when the Pudsey route closed and by March 1939 all the cars – 448 plus 'works' cars – were fitted with bow collectors. The Middleton cars were fitted with bow collectors in 1935 soon after introduction and there had been a period where mixed bow collector and pole trolley working had taken place on those routes which had been converted (see plate 32), and two lengths of bow were used, a longer one being required for cars on twenty-seven inch wheels which were lower. Occasionally such a car would be fitted with a short bow and I remember seeing No. 201, so fitted, stranded below the Briggate crossover, when reversing there, with the bow at right angles to the roof and about six inches short of the bag wire. The driver eventually overcame the problem (there was of course no car behind, or likely to be, to push) by allowing the car to run towards Boar Lane until contact was made and then accelerating towards the crossover as rapidly as possible until the bow lost contact. Luckily the impetus carried the car over the critical length but there was some spectacular arcing. Weak bow collector springs sometimes caused similar problems, but this could be overcome by pulling on the bow reversing rope, although I do remember seeing an ex-Hull car with the spring completely out of action and the bow flat on the roof. Another event I personally only witnessed once was a bow rope to break when the bow was being reversed. Drivers in Leeds habitually swung onto and off the front bumper to pull the rope, and in the rush hour in Briggate one evening I saw Driver Aisthorpe, who later drove the last car, swing on

**Plate 26** New Briggate about 1935 when the Odeon was the Paramount. Brush Chamberlain No. 2 waits to cross the Headrow

*(Copyright Yorkshire Post Newspapers)*

**Plate 27** Middleton bogie car No. 258 in lined red livery at Middleton on 14 April 1951

*(Author)*

the rope, which broke and fall on his back on the road. After some delay, an Inspector drove the car to Swinegate depot, but not before some considerable congestion had built up.

The effectiveness of the centre wire running even with standard trolley poles was demonstrated by the fact that in the year ended 31 March 1935, when only a portion of the overhead had been altered, there was a twenty-eight per cent reduction in trolley wire fractures, and in the next year a further sixty-seven per cent reduction was recorded, with a twenty-three per cent reduction in trolley dewirements. In my own twenty years experience of travel in bow collector days I do not remember being delayed by any 'overhead' problem.

During 1937 the London Midland and Scottish Railway, in the course of rebuilding the former Midland Railway portion of the City station (formerly Leeds Wellington Station) rebuilt the Queens Hotel and about the same time a major alteration was made to the tramway layout in City Square, which allowed all passenger loading to be concentrated on the centre area, leaving the peripheral roads clear for other traffic. It was with this relaying that the raised groove crossing was introduced into Leeds, the layout being provided by Hadfields. To reduce wear and noise cars ran on their flanges through the junctions, the success being such that this arrangement was used in all future major junction renewals. In the 1937 traffic situation this City Square system was acceptable, but in later years the double crossing of trams on the Lawnswood route with traffic circulating round City Square to reach Bishopsgate Street or Boar Lane caused traffic jams which needed reversal of trams and/or cars to free. During the period of reconstruction tram services terminated in various places in the city and the experience gained of operating without the benefit of through cars was mentioned in 1945–6 as demonstrating that a policy of abandoning through working and terminating public transport vehicles outside the central area was impracticable and that a bold policy of through cross city operation, with all that it entailed, was necessary.

1933 was also the year in which a major step was taken in rolling stock modernisation, with the purchase, for £3,000, of a large modern bogie car (No. 255) which entered service on 2 July. Apart from the experiment in 1900, this was the first bogie car to run in Leeds, and the whole pattern of the car was changed. Whilst the 1930 cars had modern electrical equipment and other excellent new features, they were nevertheless conventional four wheelers with quarter turn stairs, normal 'platform' arrangements and the typical lower saloon bulkheads. In the new car these features were dispensed with and the driver was given a separate small cab with a seat. Folding entrance doors opened direct into the long lower saloon; the straight staircases were internal, and on this first car they were on the opposite side to the doors. Rosewood finished were used throughout and improved upholstered

**Plate 28** 1921 built Hamilton balcony No. 350, after fitting with air and mechanical track brakes and subsequent rebuilding, at Corn Exchange 20 Sep 1949. Note the sag of the platform

*(Author)*

**Plate 29** No. 337 at the Corn Exchange 20 January 1950 shows the later body style used for three 'converts' in 1937–9. It was No. 321 until 1948

*(Author)*

seats were fitted. The buses were now painted in pale blue with three cream bands and a modified version of this was adopted for this car, comprising overall pale blue, lined in gold and white on the lower saloon panels and gold on the upstairs panels. A very wide cream band was used below the upper saloon windows, that below the lower saloon windows having the same 'gondola' effect as the 1930 cars. Both bands were lined in pale blue. The car was at first fitted with regenerative braking but electrically was otherwise conventional, with MV OK 42B cam-contactor controllers, four MV 109 35hp motors, and twenty-seven inch wheels with a 68:13 gear ratio which made it faster than any other car then in the fleet. It had the first of the new Maley and Taunton swing link equal axle bogies, of 4ft 6in wheelbase with Hoffmann Roller Bearings, giving a total wheelbase of 14 feet. The 36 foot long body was built by the Brush Electrical Engineering Company of Loughborough and had seventy seats, forty up and thirty down-stairs, with wind down windows to the saloons, twin headlights, and the indicators were moved for the first time to the centre of the panelling at the front. Leeds' now standard brakes were fitted – air and magnetic track, and air and hand parking wheel – and the total weight was 17 tons 6 cwt. For 1933 it was a truly modern car, as it discarded what had up to then generally been standard features in tramway practice. Extensive tests with it showed that very much improved schedules could be operated on the Middleton route if further similar cars were available.

The operation of the route with standard cars was not altogether satisfactory, and the committee decided that a further sixteen cars should be purchased. These were slightly modified from the experimental car, the stairs being transferred to the side adjacent to the doors, the overall wheelbase reduced to 13 feet 6 inches and the electrical equipment was brought right up to date. Metropolitan Vickers electro-pneumatic contactor control equipment was fitted, being housed in a large cabinet behind and to the left of the driver which unfortunately obstructed the forward view from the lower passenger saloon. Four GEC WT 181A 40hp high speed motors with twenty-seven inch wheels and a gear ratio of 71:14 were fitted so that the cars were very fast. Eight were built by the Brush Electrical Engineering Company (Nos. 256–63) and eight (Nos. 264–71) by the English Electric Company between February and April 1935. The Brush cars had ornamental metal bumpers above the normal bumpers and three bar lifeguards. The English Electric cars lacked the ornamentation and had two bar lifeguards. The voltage on the route was increased from 450 to 550 which gave even better performance.

The design of the experimental car was followed by that of a modern car on a four wheel truck expressly intended for routes with sharp curves. This followed the pattern of the bogie cars but had a streamlined front with a very distinctive 'vee' cream band and was painted in a similar pale blue livery. It had a new type of single indicator blind incorporating destination, route and number, positioned in the front panelling above the driver's window. A Maley and Taunton swing link truck of 8ft 6in wheelbase, with Hoffmann Roller Bearings, was fitted, with twenty-seven inch wheels, but normal 58:15 gearing whilst a field control system was used instead of the more usual resistances. This car entered service on 13 February 1935, being numbered 272, and two more were put into service in December 1935 (Nos. 273–4). These cars had, and No. 272 also later was altered to have, normal drum controllers and they were slightly different externally, being slightly more raked at the ends and lacking guttering below the roof. All of them had specially upholstered seats, those which faced forward or backward revolving instead of swinging over, and they were therefore able to be made a better shape at the back. I think it was the much improved comfort of the seats which accounted for the great popularity of these cars, for the Maley and Taunton truck was a great deal more bouncy than the P.35 or even P.22 trucks, and at their worst on the reserved tracks to Roundhay Park they could be nearly as rough as the pivotal cars. They were allocated to Headingley depot and spent most of their working time on the Lawnswood–Roundhay–Moortown routes. None of these new pale blue cars carried advertisements until about 1945–6.

Soon after entering service the new Horsfield cars were fitted with folding platform doors and two older English Electric Chamberlain cars (Nos. 82 and 87) were also dealt with, the trap doors at the stair top being removed. The transverse seats in the Horsfields were also a great improvement and two chamberlains (Brush/GEC No. 44 and English Electric No. 89) were similarly fitted. No further cars were altered, which was a pity, but these four remained as modified until withdrawn.

These proved to be the last new cars built for the time being, attention next being turned to the balcony cars which remained. A few of the pre 1906 cars, both Brush and Dick Kerr still remained, but planned route closures and the new cars envisaged the last of these withdrawn from passenger work in 1938. In 1934, therefore, only Nos. 115A–126A and 283–369, open balconied but platform vestibuled, could justify expenditure. In particular Nos. 340–69 were of 1919–23 vintage, only eleven to fourteen years old, and a design had been prepared to fully enclose them. The first seven were completed by March 1936 and the remainder during the next twelve months. In the reconstruction the stairs were replaced with half turn, the internal bulkhead was removed in the top deck and platform doors were fitted, making stair head traps unnecessary. A 'gondola' effect similar to the lower deck line of the 1930 and 1935 cars was made on the upper deck by making the panelling round the ends deeper and to avoid lengthening the roof, which was slightly shorter, the new front windows were raked back. The indicator was placed in the front panels, as on the Middleton cars, so that these cars

**Plate 30** Leeds built Horsfield car No. 152 in 1948 blue livery with cream indicator woodwork. Photographed at Roundhay 16 April 1952

*(Author)*

**Plate 31** No. 152 on 28 May 1955 at Roundhay with single blind indicator and Pullman ventilators. The livery is the final unlined red

*(Author)*

did not have front advertisements, except for a time when one for the 'Picture Post' was used which could be placed either side of the indicator. Otherwise little change was made. No. 342 was not dealt with, but No. 332, built in December 1914 and fitted later with a P.22 truck and air brakes was, and so thirty were modified in 1935–6, becoming known generally as 'converts'. Those with air and mechanical track brake equipment worked alongside the similarly equipped 1923–5 cars built totally enclosed especially on the Meanwood–Elland Road and Harehills–Beeston routes. The 'converts' were the first old cars to have the rockers painted blue rather than cream, to try and modernise their appearance.

This left only the sixty-nine 1908–15 built cars still running with open balconies. The converted cars were judged as successful, for in the report for the year 1936/7 reference was made to the benefit these cars were to the traffic department in wet weather by their seating capacity being increased. The older cars were presumably not generally in good enough condition for the simple conversion, so by December 1937 No. 321, built in April 1914, had been given a rather more thorough treatment, in that the whole platform was rebuilt and the new top deck end glazing was even more raked than the others. Flush panelled sides replaced the rockers, fan lights replaced the solid area above the vestibule windows, and the controller handles were replaced by new chrome finished ones similar to those on the GEC cars of 1930. The car was placed on a P.22 truck (officially said to come from No. 116A of 22 June 1908) with air and mechanical track and hand wheel brakes only. New bumpers and new lifeguards were also fitted.

Following this No. 116A itself was similarly dealt with although it retained the old pattern bumpers and lifeguards and was not provided with chromed controller handles. It too was placed on a P.22 truck with standard equipment. In order to take it off the duplicate list, it was renumbered 275 upon its return to service on 17 March 1938. A 1909 car, No. 119A, underwent similar rebuilding to become 276 on 6 May 1939, but was mounted on a 7ft 6ins Hurst Nelson truck, with hand and rheostatic brakes only, and BTH 510H controllers. This car also retained old style lifeguards. Of the remaining 1908–9 cars 125A was sold to Rotherham, who modernised it, and one was rebuilt as the Water car, being given the number 5 in the service list. Two were scrapped, but the others remained, seeing very little service.

Three of the cars withdrawn in 1936 were also converted to works cars, two 1904 Brush cars as Stores cars (no. .2 and 3) and one 1900 Dick Kerr car as a reciprocating rail grinder (No. 1). These three were notable in having twin headlights like the most recent passenger cars and, being single deck, had small towers on which an extra long bow collector was mounted. They retained their old motors and were rather slow. Nos. 2 and 3 could often be seen trundling along hauling two flat trucks with rails along them, rather in the manner of what in road transport is called a pole trailer. If one was on a service car, it was very unfortunate indeed to have to follow one of these for any distance, and 'shunting' was often resorted to. I well remember one having great difficulty climbing the hill at Roundhay Park and polishing the rails so much (it was a dry day!) that subsequent service cars also had the greatest difficulty in moving away from the stop. The Brill trucks on which these cars were mounted still retained their Maley mechanical and magnetic track shoes, but I do not know whether or not they were in working order.

The depots, and bus garages for that matter, came in for their share of the modernisation and rationalisation, the major item in which was the opening of Torre Road tram depot and bus garage by Lord Stamp of the London Midland and Scottish Railway Company on 8 April 1937, providing modern accommodation for eighty trams and one hundred and twelve buses, based on a gyratory system which avoided all shunting of vehicles. This allowed Donisthorpe Street to be turned over entirely to bus repair work and eventually Stanley Road tram depot to be closed. Swinegate had been further extended to accommodate 199 cars, Hunslet tram depot and the running shed at Kirkstall Road being closed in 1931. Hunslet was subsequently refurbished for use by buses in 1935, while the old Headingley depot was demolished in 1934, at a cost of £654, a new tram depot being built on the site with additional land purchased alongside for erection of a bus garage.

In 1937–8 108 older cars were fitted with Dunlopillo upholstered seats instead of wooden slats and by the start of the war only the remaining balconies, and the Hamilton bodied cars, built enclosed, remained with wooden seating. A start was also made in fitting windscreen wipers to the cars, 160 being dealt with in the first year. These were simple hand operated ones, which were manageable on a tram car as the driver did not need both hands to drive all the time as on a vehicle requiring steering. In the older cars the front window had been made to drop so that the driver could have an open space. This practice, modified in that two hinged glass slats were provided, remained standard in London, the 'Felthams' being without wipers when they came to Leeds in 1951–2. They were later modified with new one piece windscreens and wipers.

The report for 1938–9 refers to the opening of the new Central Bus Station adjacent to Quarry Hill Flats and remarks upon the fact that in order to give a frequent service to the two railway stations, the track in New York Street had been doubled and a single line laid in Harper Street to join with the old inwards line via Marsh Lane and Kirkgate which was thereafter not customarily used by normal service cars. This line was finally abandoned on 19 November 1944. It was reported that the facility was much appreciated by the travelling public, but the site of the bus station generally was not. It would be difficult to suggest where else it might have been built (even now a more convenient alternative

**Plate 32** View in Briggate in 1938 showing mixed bow collector and trolley pole working. The cars are Brush Chamberlains 30 and 27, 1928 Hamilton 407, English Electric Chamberlain 117 and Horsfield 186

*(Copyright Yorkshire Post Newspapers)*

**Plate 33** 1935 streamlined car No. 273 at Harehills on 24 April 1951. The car is in red lined livery, the lining on the top panelling being unique with this livery

*(Author)*

site would be impossible to suggest at reasonable cost) but it was hardly 'central', and a second tram or bus journey was needed to many parts of the city's commercial area.

The 1938–9 winter was not notably severe, but by now the extent of bus operation necessitated sanding of roads, the whole operation being undertaken, and the cost borne, by the unlucky transport department. The 1939–40 winter was a very severe one however, with considerable damage to rolling stock and track, the first time such events had been worthy of remark in the annual report since 1932–3.

It was at this time that the first moves were being made in the second hand tram market with more modern cars. There had been transfers from the 1920s, for instance some Sunderland and District cars went to Grimsby, but it was only when the closure of some of the larger systems which had acquired modern cars began that the desirability of obtaining such vehicles became apparent. Thus in 1938, Sunderland acquired eight Ilford cars and one experimental UCC Feltham car from the LPTB, and eight very modern cars from Huddersfield which remained in use until the closure in 1954. Leeds still had those sixty-one balcony cars in service and as the London HR2 cars were likely to become available with the abandonment of that system, arrangements were made for twenty-five to be transferred to Leeds. These were of similar vintage to the 1930 Leeds air cars and, although comparable in seating standards, they were much inferior in equipment, particularly brakes. In the event only three arrived before war conditions put a stop to replacement in London and the first was put in service in October 1939, as further described in the next chapter.

Concurrent with this improvement and modernisation of the system was the abandonment of the unsuitable routes which contained single track loop sections or ran outside the city boundary. The first replacement was from 31 January 1934 when the Hyde Park circular route was closed between Cambridge Road and Abyssinnia Road and buses substituted which later became the 57, 58, 59 and 60 circular services. Trams continued to work between City Square and Abyssinnia Road and along Cambridge Road until 5 June 1934 when these ceased without any additional bus routes being introduced. The Beeston cars which had worked to Cambridge Road were diverted to Meanwood. On 16 October 1934 buses took over the long out boundary route to Guiseley beyond the city boundary at Hawksworth Road. Through bus working was introduced from Foundry Lane and Dib Lane but later these workings were split into separate services operating from the Central Bus Station. A further outboundary route closed on 22 January 1935 when the Morley trams were cut short at Churwell Dye Works at the city boundary. Only peak hour workings in fact ran beyond Elland Road football ground. Buses in this case ran from the Corn Exchange with service numbers 52, 53, 55 and 56.

A year passed before further contraction took place when on 26 February 1936 the South Accommodation Road circular trams were replaced by buses 63 and 64 and the Lower Wortley cars which had worked there were diverted along York Road where they reversed at Harehills Lane. Soon after this they worked onto the new Gipton Estate route. It was 1 May 1937 before another change occurred when the trams from City Square to Cardigan Road via Burley Road were replaced by buses from City Square to North Lane and Beckett's Park, numbered 74, 75 and 76, but trams continued to run to North Lane via Woodhouse Lane, Victoria Road and Cardigan Road. On 14 December 1937 the associated route to Domestic Street was given to the buses, a new circular service numbered 29 being introduced. No change in services took place at the north side of the city where Domestic Street cars had continued to terminate at Victoria Road bottom, apart from the discontinuance of this point for regular reversals.

Three routes were changed to bus operation in 1938, Elland Road to Churwell Dye Works on 8 January for which no other changes were required, Bramley Town End to Rodley on 17 May and Stanningley to Pudsey on 3 December. Both the latter services had worked from the Corn Exchange and the new bus services (54 and 65 respectively) were simple replacements from the Central Bus Station. The Armley Road tram service was now a single route from Corn Exchange to Half Mile Lane Stanningley, with some peak hour workings to Cohen's Foundry at Stanningley. Route number 14 was retained.

All tram operation outside the city boundary had now ceased, but Corporation buses were working to Morley, Guiseley and Pudsey, although operation to Horsforth and Guiseley was eventually taken over by the local Tilling Group Company, the West Yorkshire Road Car Company, from 1 May 1955.

Some considerable expenditure was involved in road reinstatement, for instance costs for these works on the Guiseley and Belle Vue Road routes totalled nearly £20,000 and on the routes outside the city boundary where agreements had been entered into with other highway authorities arrangements had to be made about the payments agreed upon when the tramways were authorised.

The effectiveness of bus operation continued to improve, the superiority of the diesel engined over the petrol engined bus being acknowledged in the 1934–5 report both in economy, reliability and maintenance and by 1939 the remaining petrol vehicles were only used at the peak hours and for specials. Despite the modernisation and rationalisation of tramway operation, and the growing bus system, the 1938–9 report expressed considerable concern about the way in which costs were chasing revenue and drew attention to the effect upon this of the peak problem, especially in relation to vehicles turned out to operate only one loaded trip. This remains to the present a serious problem for all passenger transport undertakings and in the pre war days there was not the quantity of school special work to undertake which assists to some extent in the present day.

On the international front the probability of war was sufficiently great that there was a section in the 1938–9 report on air raid precautions and preparations to operate under war conditions. These preparations had to be brought into use in September 1939 and it was a significantly different transport system which entered the war era than had been in existence less than a decade before. Bus mileage had to be reduced to save fuel oil quite quickly and some routes were withdrawn for the duration of the war, thus leaving the trams to carry the bulk of the war traffic for a second time. For a second time they suffered heavy wear and a minimum of maintenance in the process.

**Plate 34** Horsfield car No. 191 waiting on the 'Stanningley' curve at the Corn Exchange, 26 April 1951. West Riding buses used the circle the opposite way. Behind is prototype Horsfield No. 154, newly painted

*(Author)*

CHAPTER 6

# The War and its aftermath 1939–48

## The war period

The construction of new cars from 1926, and the reconstruction of the 1919–23 built balconies, together with the four older ones, had brought the rolling stock to a reasonable state, the remaining balcony cars not being called upon to run very much mileage. The three London HR2 cars which came to Leeds were put into service respectively in October and December 1939, and June 1940, but their performance alongside the Leeds cars was disappointing, particularly on hilly routes, and they soon were put to work on the Hunslet route. Their main service brake was the magnetic track, but in Leeds the hand brake alone was customarily used and their accelerative capacity was not good despite the four 35hp motors. They were painted in the pale blue livery (numbered 277–9) but their appearance did not compare too favourably with most Leeds cars, as they had external indicator boxes and vestibules had been added after construction, and this was all too obvious. Otherwise they had straight body sides and upholstered seating throughout, transverse in both saloons. Wind down windows were fitted to the top deck but fan lights ventilated the lower saloon. In Leeds a normal blind replaced the stencil route number in the same box.

Tramway extension on suitable routes was still considered desirable and work on the new route to serve the Belle Isle area continued, until on 22 July 1940 a 1,300 yard extension was opened, the majority on central reservation, the overhead being supported by side poles and span wires. The cars on this extension continued to run to and from Cardigan Road via Neville Street, City Square and Hyde Park and the destination 'Belle Isle' was introduced for the new terminus, the number twenty-six being retained. 'Balm Road' (the original terminus) remained as a short working terminus. Housing and tramway development was suspended for the duration of the war after this opening.

Replacement of the sixty-one balcony cars was necessary, as war conditions required maximum use of as many cars as possible. As further London cars could not be obtained, and workshop capacity together with the condition of the cars precluded any large scale reconstruction of the balcony cars, although No. 339 of 1915 was dealt with in 1942, some other solution had to be found. The Hull system continued to be converted to trolley bus operation and its surplus cars answered the problem, thirty-two being obtained in 1942. Although these were generally old, relied on the handbrake for service use although having magnetic track brakes for emergency use, were of low seating capacity (one as low as fifty-four), they were fully enclosed and had trucks, motors and controllers similar to the old Leeds cars they were intended to replace. The first twelve entered service between February and May 1942, a further six during June and July 1942, and fourteen between October 1942 and February 1943. After this a number of balcony cars were placed 'out of service' at Torre Road and a few were put into Hunslet.

The blackout had been in force for sometime and had prompted certain minor modifications to the cars. Those with pendant lights and white shades had the latter replaced with black shades giving only a very limited beam downwards, while on cars with recessed lighting, the glass covers were painted black, giving an equally reduced lighting. Netting was stuck on the windows, as a precaution against blast damage injuring passengers, with just very small peepholes in the middle and the result was very gloomy indeed! Externally headlights were fitted with a cover to reduce the amount of light emitted, whilst to enable the cars to be seen more easily each had a broad white band painted round the dash, level with the headlight and the bumpers and steps were also painted white. Paint shortages and the shortage of staff resulted in the use of khaki grey paint from early 1942 which was entirely unrelieved by lining, edging or anything else, but the maroon trucks and lifeguards were retained. The exceptions were Horsfield cars and the pale blue cars which never had the broad white band, although grey painted Horsfields had the beading normally separating the cream band and blue panels painted white. No pale blue cars were ever painted grey and throughout the period of grey painting, odd cars – presumably those with paint in a good condition – were repainted in the blue and cream livery. The first three batches of Hull cars entered service in grey, being among the first cars so treated. Curiously they did not have the white bands on the dash.

Externally, despite the uniformity of colour, and a basic similarity of style, these Hull cars presented a surprising variety of shape, although all had domed roofs of greater or less depth. The majority had four window top decks with drop windows and four window lower saloons, but there were some of the Milnes rebuilds with three window bodies. Route number boxes and destination blind boxes were placed in three different combinations. One car (468) had a three window top deck with fan lights, stair head vestibules and a rather flatter domed roof, being the top deck of Hull 101 on the four window lower deck of Hull174. Quite a few had timber dashes and the trucks were Brill or P.22, the latter of varying wheelbase from 7ft to 7ft 6in.

After the Hull cars were put into service the balconies placed in store were not disposed of as the Ministry of War Transport imposed a ban on the breaking up of any cars and it was obviously desirable to have some spare cars in workable condition in case of an air raid resulting in a number of cars being rendered unserviceable. To make this even less likely, a number were taken out to Templenewsam, where the last section of track was singled and one running line and the loop were used to store them. Because of the tram ride, a trip to Templenewsam was a great attraction to me, as a boy, at this time, and I can clearly recall the balcony cars being stored as described above. Most were in a very sorry state, having been in the open for about two years, and not having been painted since about 1936–8. Many still carried obsolete metal plate advertisements not then to be seen on cars in the working fleet. In addition to this permanent out stabling service cars were kept out at night at Middleton, Easterly Road, Low Fields Road and elsewhere in implementation of another Ministry of War Transport directive.

An unexpected wartime benefit of the fitting of bow collectors was the ease with which they could be reversed during the blackout. An upward shining light was occasionally used to assist with putting pole trolleys on the wire, which was especially frowned upon at this period. There was of course no street lighting, which was the usual source of light, and the difficulty of finding the overhead wire must have been considerable in the many places which still retained the trolley. The Ministry advised the use of trolley pans to overcome this problem, which were so successful in Edinburgh they were retained to the end of operations.

Electric traction in general came under fire at this time because of the arcing between live wire or rail and collection equipment which was a very good guide to enemy aircraft that they were near either a railway line or urban area. A standing instruction to motormen to shut off power when passing under section insulators existed, as the flash caused by not doing so damaged both overhead equipment and collector, but their timing was not always precise, and some of the section insulators were awkwardly placed, so that arcing did take place at them. In an attempt to obviate the difficulty they were by-passed, a practice which, of course, rendered them ineffective as a means of isolating power from a certain section. In this case the Ministry recommended the placing of hoods over the section breakers.

Leeds, however, suffered very little from enemy air raids during the war, there being only one of any significance when the City railway station was hit, the museum severely damaged and some shops were

**Plate 35** The wartime livery. Brush Horsfield No. 223 outside Bramley depot

*(Copyright Leeds City Transport)*

**Plate 36** The wartime 'Austerity' car, numbered 275, in royal blue livery, on the Corn Exchange curve 19 April 1950

*(Author)*

damaged. The blast from the bombs at the station blew out windows in a number of trams in Swinegate depot and these were in service for a short time with the affected windows boarded over, but they were soon reglazed, and this was the only real damage to the Tramway system caused by enemy action.

One tramcar was, however, lost during the war period, this being English Electric Chamberlain No. 104 which caught fire between Oakwood and Roundhay Park on 3 July 1942 and was burnt beyond repair. In view of the fact that tramcars were built mainly of timber, and were electrically propelled, it is perhaps surprising that more serious fires did not occur. Minor fires were not unknown, but No. 104 was the only Leeds tramcar to be destroyed in this way.

Replacement of the car was deemed necessary and a new car was built at Kirkstall Road works, which was officially a reconstruction as new building was not permitted during the war. It was always known as the 'Austerity' car, in keeping with then current furniture, clothing, etc., and was basically similar to the 1934 streamliners, but without any of the ornamentation. It was mounted on a P.35 truck with standard Maley and Taunton air wheel and track brakes, but with thirty-two inch wheels and MV 114 motors recovered from the fire. It entered service on 11 December 1943, retaining the number 104, and was painted pale grey (not the usual wartime colour) with a white band below the upper deck windows. It was allocated to Bramley, which by then provided cars only for the 14 service Corn Exchange to Stanningley, and although moved to Swinegate when Bramley depot was closed, rarely worked on any other service until the Stanningley route was closed in 1953. Like the streamliners it had a single combined route number and destination blind from the start. The 'Austerity' was evidenced by non-upholstered seating on the top deck, and a wooden dash.

As previously described, the three London HR2 cars were not particularly successful, and in 1943 No. 277 was equipped with M and T air wheel and track braking, and platform doors, although it was not completely repainted. It returned to service on 26 June 1943 and moved to the Roundhay/Moortown–Lawnswood group of services on which it remained until withdrawn. Its performance was improved by these additions, but the positioning of the air brake cylinders adversely affected its riding, which became rather swinging.

As the war progressed conditions eased and early in 1944 blue and cream repainting was resumed, with some detail differences from the pre-war standard, and at first with the narrower white band on the dash of those classes so treated which had been introduced about 1943. The window netting was gradually removed and after blackout restrictions were withdrawn the light covers and black paint were dispensed with, although the white shades never reappeared, and soon after the glass shades on the post 1930 cars were removed to leave uncovered bulbs in all cars.

Reduced maintenance of track and trucks during the war had a particularly adverse effect on the EMB Pivotal trucks which themselves were very heavy on the track. Nearly half the cars in the fleet (200) were fitted with them, and as most of these were still less than twenty years old, it was decided in 1944 to experiment by mounting two cars on P.35 trucks, Nos. 91 and 147 being selected. No. 91 retained its thirty-two inch wheels and MV 114 motors, re-entering service on 5 August 1944, but No. 147 was additionally modified with twenty-seven inch wheels and BTH 509 motors, subsequently removed in 1948, re-entering service in July 1944, and both were painted grey, although blue painting had otherwise been recommenced. The deterioration of the EMB pivotal trucks had manifested itself in very poor riding qualities, both severe bumping and violent side oscillation. Cars fitted with them were extensively used on the Moortown–Roundhay and Lawnswood routes at this time, were the only ones normally used on the York Road group of routes, and on sleeper track had become particularly uncomfortable to ride on. The two retrucked cars exhibited none of these characteristics, and provided a very smooth comfortable ride.

It was decided to retruck all the pivotal cars and there was talk of replacing some P.22 trucks as well, although these plans were never fully realised. The transport department purchased the rights to build P.35 trucks from the Brush Company, having the capability at Kirkstall Road, and these were at first fitted to English Electric Chamberlains which retained MV 114 motors and thirty-two inch wheels. The first of these cars were No. 93, returned to service on 31 March 1945, and No. 120 on 3 May 1945. All retrucked cars were at first allocated to Torre Road depot, for use on the York Road routes which contained a large proportion of reserved track, and the regular use of 'pivotal' cars on those routes was ended by 1948, after which retrucks were sent mainly to Headingley and Chapeltown depots for use on the Roundhay–Moortown–Lawnswood routes.

From September 1945 an intensive programme was carried out, eight more cars being dealt with by the year end, thirty-two during 1946, twenty-four in 1947, thirteen in 1948 and nine in 1949. Two retrucked cars were withdrawn in 1951/2 (Nos. 59, 149) but two others were retrucked in 1951 and three in 1952, the last being No. 107. The majority were cars with MV 114 motors of the English Electric and Brush series together with three of the Leeds built cars (420/3/39), and 408 from the 1928 Hamilton style bodied cars. Four of the G.E.C. equipped cars (12, 34/8, 44) received new trucks and new WT 28 motors with twenty-seven inch wheels as did two Leeds built cars (433/4) and Hamilton bodied car 396 finished up so equipped after certain experiments in 1950. Thus 94 cars, rather less than half the pivotals, were actually dealt with, the reason that none of the Brush cars with WT 32 motors were retrucked with the existing motors not being obvious.

The Hull system was finally closed down in 1945 and the ten best cars came to Leeds, being placed in service between August 1945 and March 1946, numbered 478–87, of which 483 had top deck ventilator lights and stair head vestibules like 468. These cars entered service in standard blue and cream livery with the typical broad cream band below the upper saloon windows. The advertisements were placed in the bottom part of the top deck panelling, as was standard with Leeds cars. All the Hull cars had small shaded numerals because the headlight was so placed that the usual large numerals could not be placed either above or below it. A similar situation existed with the three London HR2 cars and No. 104. When the grey Hull cars began to be repainted blue, the positioning of the advertisements in the centre of the top deck panels precluded the provision of the broad cream band, and an unlined narrow band was used, as a simpler solution than repositioning all the advertisements. One or two (I recall 462 in particular) had this narrow band lined out.

The possibility of trams being damaged by air raid action having passed and the Ministry of War Transport embargo on scrapping having been withdrawn the bodies of the remaining balcony cars, except Nos. 302, 309, 328, 334, 338 and 342 which were officially kept in service for a little longer, were advertised in the local press for sale for £40 each. The city architect would not permit their erection within the city area, but as an additional inducement three plans were prepared by the transport department, showing alternative schemes for adapting the car body as a shed or bungalow, and these were given to the purchasers to enable them to make such alterations as they wished. Six cars (Nos. 288, 299, 317, 318, 324, 326) were sold, two (291, 313) had previously been dismantled and the bodies used for firewatching purposes, and the remainder were stripped and burnt, 337 on 23 May 1944, 293 on 20 April 1945 and the remaining forty-four between October and December 1945.

Towards the end of the war, plans for the post war period were being considered and some detailed thought was given by the transport and city engineers departments to a scheme for tramway tunnels across the central area. Plans were prepared showing the tunnel mouths, that proposed for Lower Briggate (dated 14 October 1944) being incorporated in a scheme for widening the road, the new building line providing for twenty feet of pavement and twenty-two feet of road on either side of a twenty-six foot wide tunnel mouth. The trams emerged on a rising gradient of one in fifteen against a road falling gradient of one in thirty/twenty-one.

The proposals at this time were for tunnels with 2ft 6in steel trough tops and reinforced concrete walls and floor, 16ft 6in high and 21ft 4in wide with a steel faced guide kerb to permit bus operations on a very limited clearance if required. These clearances were shown, for a 7ft 6in wide vehicle, as 2ft 0in wall to vehicle, and 2ft 3in between vehicles. One drawing showed a profile of a bus in the tunnel, and another a standard 1930 car (at 6ft 11in wide) alongside a proposed single decker (numbered 510 and 7ft 6in wide) with two piece front driving cab windows, rather similar to cars 272–4.

The intention was to have 'stations' at focal points, under the Headrow near Wade Lane, under Briggate near Commercial Street and under the Corn Exchange area beyond the surface turning circle. A drawing of the proposed City Square station showed the additional platform space to be 10ft wide, slightly raised with 8ft headroom, but a longitudinal girder at the tunnel side reducing headroom to 6ft 9in. The means of access from street level was not described.

Apart from Lower Briggate, entrances to the tunnel system were proposed for Wellington Street, near Queen Street, Woodhouse Lane near Blackman Lane, New York Street before St. Peters Street and North Street just before Skinner Lane, so that the underground system would have covered an area very similar to that proposed in 1895 for conduit working. An interesting inference to be drawn from this is that although the city had expanded very much in the intervening fifty years, the compact central area remained very similar in extent, and the same is true today nearly another half century later.

An insurmountable difficulty in this scheme was the sub-soil and the presence of a variety of services, sewers, cables etc., making cut and cover construction quite impracticable, so attention was turned to a tube scheme, which was developed initially over a similar area but was later reduced in extent. This scheme would not have permitted double deck vehicles. In part 8 of his series 'Leeds Trams 1939–59' in *Modern Tramway* (February 1973 and subsequently published in book form by the Light Rail Transit Association) Andrew Young describes in detail the work of the City Council's Reconstruction Committee, which considered the schemes as part of a broader examination, from verbatim accounts of proceedings he had located. The Committee was wound up and these far sighted plans were filed away.

A positive move connected with this scheme was made in 1944 when Sunderland car No. 85 was purchased. This was an end platform bogie single decker of considerable length, mounted on maximum traction bogies. Leeds replaced these with EMB Heavyweight bogies of the type on the three HR2 cars in service, and numbered the car 288, presumably about 1946. It was painted plain grey and only ventured out on a few night time clearance tests. Plans were made to rebuild it into a centre exit car with tapered ends and modern equipment, which did eventually come to fruition in 1954, although EMB Heavyweight 'Johannesburg' bogies were used. The car eventually went to the Crich Museum after being withdrawn in 1957.

The problems of providing any kind of immediately sub-surface subway, even for pedestrians, in the city centre remain and future segregation of traffic and pedestrians is provided for by pedestrian precincts and, in the sixties, by raised walkways, a concept now happily abandoned. The far sighted tunnel scheme which would have put Leeds well ahead in public transport development did not therefore materialise and the consequent abandonment policy leaves long lengths of dual carriageway reservation unused, with the adjacent roads more congested by the buses. The early nineties are seeing a great debate to determine new transport policies, which may include a street-rail option, which would have been unnecessary if wiser counsels had prevailed in the late forties.

## Post war developments

The war period had placed a great strain on the tramway system, the situation not being helped by there being some 1,400 employees in HM Forces throughout the years 1940–5. The increase in the use of public transport caused by the restrictions (especially petrol rationing) on the use of private cars and the increase in the numbers of people actually working for the war effort had been borne by the trams more than the buses, services operated by the latter having been curtailed or even withdrawn to save fuel oil. The measure of this is demonstrated by the number of passengers carried on the undertaking in the year ended 31March 1945 of 232,605,776 which was 32, 321,112 more than the year ended 31 March 1939. Arrears of car maintenance and track repairs continued to increase, and a deficit of £43,535 was reported for the year.

The following year a 10,000,000 reduction in passengers carried was recorded, being less than expected, and the deficit rose to £74,563. There was a remarkable parallel with conditions at the end of the first world war when a shortage of Portland cement caused a severe hold up of track repair and renewal work. This time rails were the problem and no new ones were delivered for ten months, recovery from abandoned sections having to be resorted to to undertake urgent repair work.

There was a deficit again in 1946–7 of £189,556, and after a fares revision in 1945 a public enquiry was held and a new fares structure was approved and introduced on 2 March 1946 which maintained the balance for the next two years, but the respite was only temporary. In 1947 the forty-four hour week was introduced from 6 April but, as the staff position precluded its actual implementation, a considerable additional cost was incurred by having to retain the forty-eight hour

**Plate 37** Ex-Hull car No. 131 as Leeds No. 457, after painting blue, at Roundhay 2 Aug 1948

*(Author)*

**Plate 38** English Electric Chamberlain No. 138 in Briggate rush hour in 1946. The other cars are LCT Chamberlain 420 (in pre-war livery) 'Convert' 360 and LCT Chamberlain 445

*(Copyright Yorkshire Post Newspapers)*

rosters and paying overtime for the difference. Unhappily, for those who favoured tramcars, this was only the beginning.

Leeds, like other cities in Great Britain, had by 1945 a considerable housing problem and a major extension of the urban area again became necessary, both to cope with the now increased demand for houses and to pursue the pre-war policy of slum clearance. The two main areas of the city selected before the war were now rapidly expanded by municipal building. The existing Belle Isle tram route ran to the pre-war limit of extensive building along Belle Isle Road, although a bus service had run to Broom Estate at the South East extent of the city, but the Seacroft area was insufficiently developed to warrant a service. The Seacroft tram service was considered in the mid-thirties, but apart from the short length in Gipton Approach opened in 1936 little had been done. After the 1940 opening to Belle Isle, powers had been obtained in 1941 for a further extension, and in 1945 for the link up to the Middleton route.

At this time buses were difficult to obtain. For example, the report for year ended 31 March 1946 recorded seventy-five buses had been allocated but were not expected to be delivered until 1947, and although in March 1946 tenders had been invited for new tramcars, without any acceptable response, it was intended to continue the policy of expanding reserved track routes and abandoning unsuitable single track sections. The city council, therefore, took a policy decision to retain the tram as the principal trunk service vehicle.

Building work took place first at Belle Isle and, in line with the above policy, work on extending the tram route was pressed on, the six furlongs authorised in 1941 being completed on 2 February 1946. Regular service started on 24 February. Thereafter work continued on linking up with the Middleton route and the section up Belle Isle Ring Road was opened on 6 March 1949, from when the route No. 27 was used to denote journeys running to that point as distinct from the older terminus. The remainder was soon completed and circular working commenced on 28 August 1949, the descriptions 26 circular and 12 circular being introduced with the destination 'Middleton' used by cars operating in both directions. The Belle Isle section was on central reservation, followed by a short section built in advance of the road, then on side reservation along the Ring Road to join with the original section at Middleton. The overhead was supported by side poles and span wires and the rails were set in concrete, as used in Gipton Approach in 1936, rather than the older sleeper and ballast construction. A three line layout was made at Middleton to accommodate cars terminating there via the express route. The sixteen 1935 bogies cars still maintained most of the services, but 1930 Horsfield cars were more in evidence than previously.

The Seacroft extension, however, was not proceeded with. By the time a transport need was created by building progress buses were available to work to Seacroft and the service was gradually strengthened as required thereafter, until it now is incorporated in the Pudsey/Bramley–Seacroft group of services which is one of the busiest in the city.

In 1945 three tram services remained which incorporated single line sections and, to complete the pre-war policy of abandoning such sections, they were replaced by buses as rapidly as possible. Services 11 to Harehills Road (via Beckett Street) and 19 to Lower Wortley were abandoned on 25 August 1946 and replaced by a new through bus service 42 Harehills to Lower Wortley, via the Headrow. Previously the Harehills Road trams had worked through from and to Dewsbury Road, and the Lower Wortley ones Gipton Estate. To balance matters, through working began after the withdrawals between Dewsbury Road and Gipton Estate, which took Hull cars onto the York Road reserved track section regularly for the first time. From 15 September 1946, the Gipton route number was altered from 21 to 11 to reduce the amount of indicator blind winding required. Service 27 to Cardigan Road via Hyde Park was withdrawn beyond Hyde Park from 7 December 1947 and the route covered by a new bus service. The trams continued to run through between Hyde Park and Belle Isle (via Neville Street) and the bus service introduced was 56 from the central bus station via Moorland Road and Victoria Road to Cardigan Road terminus, which was from then known as North Lane.

There was no general withdrawal of cars following these changes, as the extension to Belle Isle had to some extent provided a balance, and in any event the repair situation was so poor that there had been some shortage of service tramcars during 1947, and Saturday morning working had been resorted to in order to ease the position. It was not therefore politic to reduce the fleet, although the remaining balcony cars, except 309, and ex-Hull cars 471/6, had been withdrawn during 1946–7.

During the war the practice of fixing advertisements to the exterior of the cars by bolting enamelled plates had given way to the use of paper and also to direct painting onto the car. The latter was more successful, as the paper ones faded and also became dislodged. As a small boy I well remember going to the reserved track near the Gipton Hotel to pick up a complete 'Victory will be sweeter with Mars' advertisement which had come off some car.

The painting out of advertisements applied directly onto the car required the lining out being replaced, which was a rather time wasting and expensive operation, and was soon discontinued. In new repaintings, in order to maintain a better appearance, the lining was left off the upper deck panelling from early in 1947, as described in Appendix A dealing with liveries.

Despite the progress in retrucking the pivotal cars and overhauling and repainting of other cars, it was clear that there were a number of cars which needed replacement. The travelling public was no longer content to be bounced, shaken and swung as they had been on 6ft 6in wheelbase Brill and Hurst Nelson or even 7ft 6in wheelbase P.22 trucks. These had no doubt been adequate for the shorter, lighter cars, often uncanopied and at best with open balconies to the top deck, of years ago, but the longer overhang of totally enclosed cars and the greater weight of that overhang caused these trucks to give a very unstable ride, to which their considerable age by 1948 added. The bodywork of the 1935–6 balcony conversions was in poor shape, particularly the very characteristic sagging of the platforms, and the Hull cars were also the subject of criticism. Many of the older cars also had wooden seats, a point not appreciated by the travellers on the routes on which they were regularly used, although these seats were well shaped and not too uncomfortable.

Second hand cars were not new to Leeds – the London HR2 with air brakes was quite popular and although the Hull cars were not it was generally accepted that they were better than the balcony cars they replaced – so when Manchester decided to sell their thirty-eight 1930 'Pilcher' or Pullman cars, one was obtained. This was No. 287, placed in service in Leeds on 3 August 1946, painted grey and retaining its Manchester number (in Manchester style numerals). I first saw it on the No. 11 service Harehills Road–Dewsbury Road, and it worked from Swinegate depot always. These cars were a cross between old and modern, in that they had a modern looking domed roof top deck with drop windows, and incorporating curved glass at the ends. Internally they had upholstered transverse seating throughout, and were finished in medium oak rather than the very dark colour usual on trams. The lower deck, however, had the usual fan lights and rocker panels, and the setting of the fan lights gave a very old fashioned appearance. The car had a P.35 truck, but with plain bearings, and it had only hand and magnetic track brakes. Twenty-seven inch wheels were fitted, with MV 105 motors, and a high gear ration of 62:13 made it fast in service. It was regarded as sufficiently successful to justify the purchase of more, but other undertakings had been quicker making the decision and only six remained available. These came to Leeds in 1948.

During 1947–8, alongside the work of keeping the fleet in as good condition as possible, a new car was being built (albeit slowly) at Kirkstall Road works. This was a double decker based on the same lines as the pre-war streamliners and the 'austerity' car, but with some rounding of the sharp corners of the latter, and lacking the heavy ornamentation of the former. It was mounted on a P.35 truck with WT28S motors, twenty-seven inch wheels and M and T air wheel, air and magnetic track brakes, and BTH 510N controllers. Internally it was polished in light oak throughout and had upholstered seating, but with swing over non-upholstered backs. It was numbered 276 and entered service on 20 September 1948.

Before it was completed Mr. V. J. Matterface took over the post of rolling stock engineer, and it was about this time that I first obtained permission to visit Kirkstall Road works and met him. After this time some considerable changes were made in livery and equipment, and from June 1948 until abandonment was announced in 1953 there was a period of very great interest to the observer.

**Plate 39** Duncan Street, with the Corn Exchange dominating the background on Sunday 18 May 1952. The work was to the road surface, not the track. The cars are English Electric Chamberlain No. 123 and Horsfield No. 193.

*(Author)*

CHAPTER 7

# The final developments

The most obvious change was in livery, and this was aimed at reducing the difficulty experienced keeping the cream bands clean. No important change in the painting style – except perhaps the cessation of painting the rocker panels cream – had taken place since 1930, although a gradual simplification had been effected up to 1942, but in the five years 1948–53 the variety of liveries used was remarkable. Certain of the experiments were not found satisfactory and were not perpetuated, one such being the painting of the indicator box woodwork cream rather than brown on a number of cars in the last half of 1948. Experience showed that the light paint had an adverse effect upon the clarity of the destination blinds and the brown paint was re-introduced, although some of the cream cars were finally withdrawn so painted as late as 1953. Apart from this, the various experimental liveries are described in the Appendix on liveries, but the new standard evolved was dark blue panelling, lined in deep yellow on the lower deck, with simplified corners, and cream window frames. The usual black edging was applied between blue and cream and the guttering, trucks, fan light windows and indicators were brown. It must be said that this gave a more modern appearance, but looked rather sombre. After the first few cars the large shaded numerals used on all cars except the Hull, streamlined and London cars were replaced by very clear small gill sans type and side numbers were omitted from Horsfield, Middleton bogie, streamlined and London cars.

Those cars which had pneumatic bells (those built after 1930) had very large and ugly bell pushes, with the bell operated from upstairs and down. The older cars had cord bells downstairs, running through the standing strap supports, and conductors signalled from upstairs by whistle, so that the driver was able to tell whether the conductor was on the platform or not. To give the driver this information, pneumatic bell cars which were given major body overhauls were provided with modern style pushes operating a bell electrically from downstairs and a buzzer from upstairs. The first car so altered was ex-London HR2 No. 277 which was returned to service in June 1948 and was also the first car to be painted in the very striking new version of the pale blue livery. As described earlier 'special' cars had been painted pale blue since No. 255 of 1933 and this was continued, but the cream bands were dispensed with as on the other cars. This new livery was a rather purer shade of pale blue with cream window frames and brown trucks or bogies and, on Nos. 277 and 258, black edging, although subsequent cars had brown edging. Deep yellow lining was applied round the dash only. Internally ceilings were painted overall white, rather than pale cream, the brown cross beading being painted white also and on 277 the white was extended in the lower saloon to include the fan lights and in the upper saloon the cornice. It was completely re-upholstered in blue moquette and fitted with an air whistle to give warning of approach, as also was the new car No. 276. It had been working from Chapeltown on the Moortown–Roundhay–Lawnswood routes since being fitted with air brakes in 1943 and returned there when this overhaul was completed. It succeeded in catching the public eye and was held in high regard for some time.

The extension of white ceiling paint was tried on some other cars but the difficulties of keeping it clean were such that it was not standardised. However the cars altered (Nos. 112, 195 I remember particularly) were not altered back.

In order to give continuity of numbering for possible additions to the fleet certain rebuilt balconies and the 'austerity' 104 were renumbered during the summer of 1948, 275 becoming 349, 276 becoming 342, 321 becoming 337 and 332 becoming 338, thus containing all the rebuilt balconies in the series 337–69, whilst 104 became 275 giving building order progression through 272–6. Enquiries had been made about the building of a batch of cars similar to No. 276 but it proved impossible to proceed as described in the previous chapter and the possibilities for obtaining more second hand cars were considered again.

At this time a major classification scheme was devised, of which I was fortunate to be given a car by car copy by Mr. Matterface, in which all the cars were described by a letter/number system similar to the LNER locomotive and London Tram schemes. Thus the remaining balconies became A1, the non air brake converts A2, the M and T air brake converts A3, and the EMB ones A3/2. No. 339 which was an A2 had been given a P.22 truck instead of Hurst Nelson and had a 'special' classification of A3/RHEO, indicating that it varied from standard A3 by having rheostatic brakes only: it might equally well have been A2/P22. Full details are given in the appendix at the rear of the book but certain inconsistencies are worth noting here.

The scheme took no account of body variations as a general rule, so that the later converts were not distinguished from the others, rebuilt

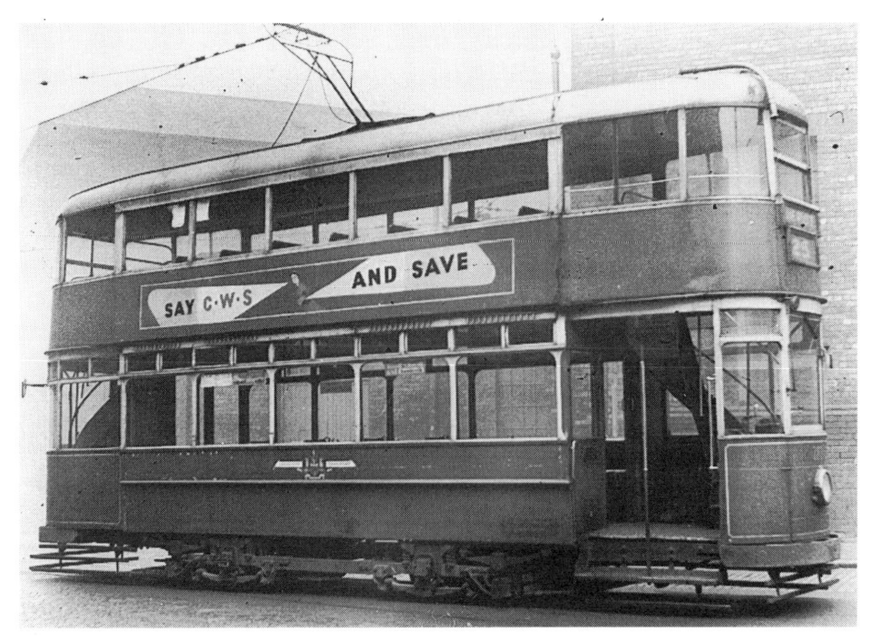


**Plate 40** Ex-Manchester 'Pilcher' car No. 266 as Leeds No. 283 in its first pale blue livery in Sovereign Street

*(Copyright Leeds City Transport)*

**Plate 41** Brush Chamberlain No. 44 with P.35 truck (27″ wheels) at Roundhay 16 Apl 1950

*(Author)*

balconies with EMB air brakes were classified A3/2 the same as electrically similar cars built totally enclosed, one 1928 Hamilton bodied car was classified B3, and the rest B3/2 along with the Leeds built Chamberlains. Similarly no distinction was made between P.35 and pivotal truck cars in Class B1, B2, B3, B3/2, nor between plain and Hoffmann bearing fitted pivotal cars. Again no distinction was made between Hoffmann and Skefko roller bearings on Horsfield cars, and all the London cars were F1, although 277 had air brakes.

By contrast Middleton bogies D2 and D3 differed only in being Brush and English Electric built, and Beeston air brakes (built totally enclosed) A3/2 only differed from A3/3 by having DB1 K3 controllers instead of DB1 K4B. No. 78 which for a time had a roller bearing P.22 truck (referred to as 'Edinburgh') was classified B2/3 rather than B2/P22 as might have been expected, whereas No. 147 was originally B2/27/BTH/5815 (i.e. 27in wheels, BTH 509 motors, 58:15 gearing) when all other 27in wheel retrucks were given a sub class (i.e. Nos. 12, 34, 38 and 44 Class B1/3; 433/4 Class B3/3).

But it was a classification scheme and did confirm and identify many oddities which I had observed; it must have been a major job as the letters reached J (Nos. 275, 276) and the number of 'special' classifications was considerable. For a few years any alterations were shown on the cars' painted classification, which at first was placed at the left hand bottom corner of the rocker or side panel when they were repainted. After June 1952 (84 was the first car) a plate was fixed to the bulkhead behind the stairs, and it was from this time that alterations stopped being made, although a number of cars in fact were so altered electrically that they changed classes – for instance Brush/GEC Chamberlains (B1/2) 24, 28, 29, 39 all finished their days with OK9B controllers and MV114 motors which made them standard B1. Officially they never changed but the appearance of controllers and the sounds of motors were quite distinctive and the observer was well able to know what had been done without an official reclassification.

In general, however, the cars continued to be known by the familiar names which various people had devised for them, in contrast to London, from where the idea stemmed, and where the classifications were sufficiently long standing for E1, E3 and HR2 cars to be very familiarly known throughout the country among those interested in trams. The former London No. 1 and the single deckers were never classified at all, whilst the 'Feltham' cars retained their London classifications of UCC/1 and UCC/2.

Tramcar maintenance had fallen from its pre-1939 standard during the war but by 1949 much of the leeway had been recovered, and under Mr. Matterface's direction a systematic repair organisation was established. Cars were called into the works every eighteen months for a partial overhaul which consisted of a complete check of all the electrical and mechanical equipment and the bodywork, any necessary attention being given where required. Eighteen months later the car was recalled for a complete overhaul, whatever its condition. Considerable work was also done in overhauling and updating the workshop machinery. The equipment was comprehensive and the capability existed to make almost anything required for tramcar repair or construction.

The six additional Manchester cars had arrived and after much needed overhaul were placed in service between September and December 1948, as Nos. 281–6, all being painted in the new pale blue livery with silver roofs and looking very striking. No. 287 had been painted in standard dark blue and cream in March 1948, at the same time being renumbered 280. Nos. 281–2 were sent to work on the Roundhay–Moortown–Lawnswood group of services, but although they had P.35 trucks, these had plain bearings and not having been particularly well maintained, were prone to considerable oscillation. On the reserved track sections this was so bad that there were strong complaints which resulted in the cars being sent to Swinegate for use on routes with less sleeper reservations, notably non circular workings to Belle Isle.

During a visit to Kirkstall Road works at this time, I was talking to the staff there about these cars and they said there had been so many complaints about No. 287 before its overhaul in March that it had been called into works and in order to evaluate the strength of these a test was arranged along Kirkstall Road with staff as passengers. The car was driven fast and the test was soon concluded when those riding upstairs refused to stay there unless the car was driven more slowly! Truck overhauls did little to improve matters and the facts that they were a little longer than Leeds' P.35 trucked cars and rather fast both tended to aggravate the position.

Some further depot and garage rationalisation took place in 1949–50, when Bramley depot was closed on 30 January 1949 for conversion to accommodate sixty-one buses with an outside 'overflow' for fourteen more, being reopened on 4 December 1949. The new Leylands 340–99 were allocated there when new and except for a few working from Torre Road from time to time remained there until withdrawn progressively from 1964–8. The use of Kirkstall Road as a bus garage was discontinued from 15 April 1950 and it became exclusively the tramway repair shop.

The need to obtain second-hand cars still remained and the Southampton system was closing down and releasing the characteristic domed roof 'Bargate' cars, of which a number were purchased. The first one was placed in service on 6 June 1949, numbered 290 and classified K1. It was in the pale blue livery, apple green and cream inside, with

**Plate 42** Post war car No. 276 when quite new in its first pale blue livery at Roundhay 9 April 1949

*(Author)*

**Plate 43** Ex-Southampton car No. 109 as Leeds No. 291 at Kirkgate in royal blue livery, 20 Sept 1949

*(Author)*

rather austere transverse seating and very small windows in the upper saloon. External appearance was very distinctive, with a very deep domed roof and smooth side panels slightly wider at window level than at the bottom, giving a maximum width of 7ft 6in. The original 1923 cars had rocker panels, but none of these entered service in Leeds. Metro-Vick electrical equipment with small wheels and a Hoffmann Roller bearing P.35 truck with hand and rheostatic brakes only made the car electrically and mechanically very similar to the Leeds P.35 Chamberlains with small wheels. In an article *'Remember Leeds trams', A. K. Terry describes how this car was painted in Southampton before being moved to Leeds so that it would not look too decrepit on arrival.

Thirty-eight cars were actually purchased but the condition of the bodies became progressively worse, and later ones lacked essential equipment. In the event only ten more were overhauled, becoming Nos. 291–300, and when I wrote to the Transport Department asking about any more, they reported that the placing of them in service was in 'abeyance'. The others were painted in the royal blue standardised for all cars (including the former pale blue ones) from 3 July 1949, except for 299 which entered service on 20 October 1950 in the new red livery, as described later. No. 300 entered service on 16 December 1950, having been painted in the older blue and cream on 27 July 1950. The last three cars (298–300) had Skefko roller bearings and, along with No. 296, two and one fully upholstered seating and were rather more comfortable to sit in. The first car retained its separate destination blinds and route number, the latter being of a non standard size for Leeds, and was operated from outside the saloon, the conductor having to put his hand through a very small sliding opening. The remainder, however, entered service with a new type of single blind indicator incorporating destination and route number, as described later in this chapter.

There had been talk again of more London HR2 cars coming to Leeds, as originally intended in 1939, and as abandonment was under way again in London negotiations were re-opened. Leeds was able to assist London by lending some buses and as a consequence was offered a Feltham car as a sample, with a view to purchasing these. A new type of destination blind would be necessary for these cars and it was designed ready to fit to the sample car, being adopted as a standard at the same time. It was this that was fitted to the Southampton cars and soon afterwards Brush/Metro-Vick Chamberlain No. 60 was modified to accommodate this design of blind by taking out the route number portion of the standard type, glazing the space and fitting the new blind in the portion previously occupied by the destination and route blinds.

*_Tramway Memories – ed. J. Joyce – Ian Allan Ltd._

This was a great improvement in appearance both internally and externally, although the route number was considerably smaller and not visible from as far.

The sample 'Feltham' left London in September and after arrival was repainted in London livery with the standard Leeds insignia on the sides. It retained its London number (2099) and was completely repolished in light oak inside retaining the brown moquette upholstery. It entered service in Leeds on 17 December 1949 and underwent extensive trials on all routes – I travelled on it during December and January 1949–50 to Bramley, on the Roundhay circle and round the Middleton circle via Belle Isle – the most memorable part being the climb up to Belle Isle from the old Balm Road terminus. These cars had Metro-Vick OK 33B contactor controllers and EMB maximum traction bogies, and the contactor equipment had its own overload trip, so that if the controller handle was moved too fast through the notches, power was cut off without blowing the main circuit breaker. In attempting to climb the hill beyond Balm Road the driver was unable to bring the controller beyond the first notch (motors in series and all resistances but one in circuit) without tripping the contactor overload. This very slow and halting progress caused a loss of time which the driver tried to make good by hurrying down through Middleton Woods. Although 2099 was in good condition at this time, at high speed on sleeper track some severe bumping developed, in marked contrast to the performance of the 'Middleton Bogies' on this route. Generally, however, the car made a favourable impression in the city and ultimately went to Torre Road to work on the York Road routes. Apart from the early experimental bogie car of 1900, which was soon put on a Brill four wheel truck, this was the first maximum traction bogie car to operate in Leeds and although the idea of such bogies was to improve adhesion, experience in Leeds was that these cars were not good hill climbers and they suffered badly from slipping on the start, despite their 17 tons weight. This was not helped by their having flexible sand pipes held in front of the bogies by a metal ring, so that they were supposed to sand the rail whether the car was on a curve or not. This rarely happened and often on curves the car would be slipping badly, whilst a pile of sand was deposited alongside the rail. The sand was applied by air valve supplied by a hand pump, which did not endear itself to drivers and cases of cars stalling through slipping trying to climb out of lower Briggate, for example, were not unknown.

The introduction of a large batch of cars of as great a length of body and wheel base as the Feltham's for general use was made possible by the realignment of junctions which had been carried out in the post war period in preparation for use of 44 foot bogie cars as proposed in the various tunnel schemes. The works had been able to cope with the 17 Middleton cars, but to handle up to 90 more, some alterations had to be made. The space formerly used for the bus running shed had become available for this purpose after the completion of Bramley as a bus garage as described earlier.

The Leeds cars themselves did not escape improvements during and after 1948, apart from livery changes, many Chamberlain cars being completely re-upholstered in blue moquette and a start was made in replacing the top deck drop windows on the Horsfield class with larger frames incorporating Pullman sliding ventilators in alternate windows each side, starting with the one adjacent to the stair top. The full drop of the old windows had quite quickly been stopped by fixing the frame with a gap about one and a half inches at the top. The new frames closed this gap, which was beneficial both for draughts and internal cleanliness, and they were also of new light oak wood which enhanced the internal appearance. This work was normally included in body overhauls and accompanied by fitting of buzzers and new bells, and after late 1949 new style single blind indicators on these cars were also usually of new light oak wood on the inside. Two cars (191, 204) had the ventilators in the two centre windows on each side.

In the early part of 1949 the standard dark blue was replaced on some cars by a slightly brighter shade and from July by a very striking royal blue. Blue was used as previously for panelling, cream for window frames with black edging and brown for trucks and guttering. Deep yellow lining was used for the dash and side panels only. I consider this to have been the most striking livery used for Leeds cars, although there are many who will not share that opinion. All the classes painted pale blue were altered to this style, except the 1935 streamliners which were painted in the new shade of blue, but retained the cream bands as formerly, still lined out. An interesting oddity was that none of the ex London HR2 cars was ever painted in this style, all passing from pale blue to red. The blue did not, however, wear well and as more London cars were going to be transferred it was decided to paint the trams red, in an endeavour to reduce painting costs by using less expensive paint and obtain a more lasting result. The buses were changed to green at the same time for the same reasons, whilst bus and tram stops were thereafter distinguished by these colours.

During March and April 1950 a major re-allocation of cars took place in order to give each depot an allocation in numerical order. Hitherto cars had been allocated by types, but at random so far as numbers were concerned. The re-allocation included one or two novel features in that Horsfield air cars 249–54 were sent to Torre Road which had not previously had such cars and as the blocks were at first rigidly applied a number of pivotal trucked cars were sent to Torre Road, while Headingley and Chapeltown received an increased allocation of them. The only exceptions to the 'blocks' were the Southampton cars, then being placed in service, and the 'Austerity' 275 which remained at Swinegate. The allocation was as follows:

Swinegate
1–50, 143–200, 217–48, 255–71, 275, 278–86, 290/4/5, 337/9/49/50/2/9, 370/2/4–80/2–99, 400–22, 446/8/9/52–8/62–5/70–4/8–82/4–6.
Chapeltown
51–70, 201–10, 423–32.
Headingley
71–92, 211–6, 272–4/6/7/92/3.
Torre Road
93–103/5–42, 249–54, 291, 433–45, 2099.

At this time Chapeltown and Headingley depots jointly provided cars for services 1, 2 and 3 Lawnswood–City–Moortown and Roundhay, including short workings to Chapeltown and Moortown, but not to Harehills and Roundhay, Torre Road provided cars for services 15, 16, 17, 18, 20, 22 Whingate and New Inn to Harehills Lane, Crossgates and Halton and City–Templenewsam, and Swinegate provided the rest. After a few months some pivotal cars at Headingley, Chapeltown and Torre Road were replaced by P.35 cars from Swinegate, especially in the 1–10 batch, but these were changed from time to time.

From the summary of the fleet given above it will be noted that most of the rebuilt balconies, fifteen Hull cars and three of the 1923–4 enclosed cars had been withdrawn since the end of the war. Odd withdrawals had taken place – Hull cars 471/6 and balconies 302/42 during 1946, balconies 328/38 and rebuilt balcony 349 in 1947 and rebuilt balconies 345/56 and the last balcony 309 during 1948. Of these only 309/28/45 were classified in the 1948 scheme, 309 having been scheduled for preservation, 328 still existing as a stores car at Swinegate and 345 being withdrawn shortly after the scheme was finished. The remaining cars were all withdrawn between June and August 1949, except 473 which was taken out of service on 2 December, and the trucks and motors of nineteen were sold to Calcutta, fifteen of them P.22s. This amounted to a considerable reduction in the fleet since against fifty-two cars withdrawn only fifteen cars had been added to the fleet since the last batch of Hull cars arrived in 1945–6 and this was made possible by improved availability of cars together with reductions in peak short workings in their turn made possible by reduction in passengers and the shift in population.

At the time the depot reallocation was made the practise of indicating a car's home depot by letter was begun, C, H, S or T being painted after the number and class on the side panel thus:

CLASS B1<br>CAR No.71 H

The first car so treated was No. 427 in April 1950 and the letters continued to be painted after cars had been re-allocated and even after depots had been closed in later years.

**Plate 44** Ex-London HR2 car No. 1883 as Leeds No. 278 after fitting with air wheel brakes, platform doors and single blind indicators. Photographed at Roundhay 21 April 1951 in experimental vermilion livery

*(Author)*

**Plate 45** Leeds built Chamberlain No. 425 at Roundhay 11 April 1952, in red livery

*(Author)*

The story of the last balcony car to be in service is worth comment and in his article A. K. Terry describes how it was kept going on the assumption it would be withdrawn when it broke down. It would not break down, however, and eventually received some press attention, in consequence of which it was withdrawn and stored at Torre Road along with one or two converted balconies which had broken trucks as a result of the very severe winter of 1946–7 or being driven by volunteers during the strike in September 1945. I remember 354 was one of these and 339 was placed on its P.22 truck for this reason. However, in the summer of 1948, it was decided that good use could be made of 309, if it was restored to its 1914 condition and was used for special occasions. It was therefore moved to Kirkstall Road and examined, but was found to be in too poor a condition to justify such expenditure. No. 328 was still at Swinegate, however, and the bodywork was found to be in quite reasonable condition, so that this car was restored, as 309, to the old primrose, white and maroon livery, with period advertisements, and a wonderful job was done. Its place as Swinegate workshop was taken by convert No. 345, which thus survived to go to the National Tramway Museum at Crich. It was thus more fortunate than 309, which was in need of a further overhaul by August 1951 and offered to the tramway societies for a nominal sum provided they were able to have it removed. Leeds had housed Southampton No. 45 for a short time, but was not prepared to do this kind of thing again. No alternative site could be found, and very unhappily the offer had to be declined. No. 309 went to Cohen's for scrap on 3 October 1951.

The riding of the Manchester cars was still causing great concern and at the end of 1949, Nos. 285–6 were fitted with Skefko roller bearing axle boxes (and WT28S motors). This simple change brought a marked improvement to the riding, even when they again became run down, and virtually eliminated the dreadful oscillation. A third one, No. 281, was mounted on an EMB flexible axle truck of 9ft wheelbase with MV116 motors purchased from Liverpool, and this was also a great success. Nos. 281/6 were later allocated to the Roundhay–Moortown–Lawnswood group of routes again. A similar EMB truck was fitted to Hamilton car 396 at the same time but in May 1950 this was transferred to Horsfield No. 179, with the addition of rubber packed wheels to reduce track noise and rubber packed hornways to reduce transmission noise. An improved air brake valve was also fitted and the car was stripped and repolished internally in medium oak, fitted with Pullman ventilators, buzzers, bells and a single blind indicator mounted in the top of the centre front window rather than the bottom. This did not improve the appearance, and was not repeated on any other car. The result was a very smooth, steady, silent car, which compared very favourably with any other road transport vehicle at that time. No. 396 acquired a P.35 truck and 27in wheels with WT28 motors in exchange.

Ticket issuing had since 1937 been by the normal method of individual ticket punched for boarding stage and held on a spring-clip rack. Fare increases and associated reduction in stage lengths had created problems in the numbers of tickets required and a change was made in 1949/50 to Ultimate machine ticket issue, which lasted until the late '70s. One effect of this in the early stages was the transfer away from Headingley of the streamliners because the high seat backs obstructed conductors with the new machines, which were first used on the Lawnswood–Moortown–Roundhay group of services. These cars therefore appeared on Swinegate workings and 272 worked from Torre Road for a time. As the Ultimate machines came to be used more extensively, these three cars were fitted with new seats, 273 receiving a longitudinal seat right along one side of the lower deck, which were much less comfortable than the old and really spoilt them. They then returned to Headingley.

The first Leeds cars to be painted red appeared in traffic in the summer of 1950 and these included the first six London 'Feltham' cars, a number of experimental styles being used which are described in the Appendix on liveries. By October a standard had been settled on, with minor variations to suit different types of car, comprising crimson panelling and window frames, with cream bands below upper and lower window frames, fully lined out in deep yellow and red and edged in black. Brown indicator and ventilator window woodwork was retained, with brown trucks, but black guttering. Newly painted cars looked very striking indeed. Following the successful trials with No. 2099 the 'Feltham' cars had eventually been purchased from London and from September 1950 were placed in service steadily, the Metro-Vick/BTH equipped ones being sent first receiving classification UCC/1 and numbers from 502. They were allocated to Torre Road to work on the York Road sleeper track routes, displacing P.35 Chamberlains which in turn displaced 'pivotals' to the duties formerly covered by converts and ex-Hull cars. These cars were thoroughly repolished inside in light oak and the annual report recorded that the 'modern interior finish of the UCC cars entails much labour and effort'. They entered service more or less in numerical order the last being on the road in September 1951, numbers 521/3/50. As the freshly overhauled ones were being brought out the earlier ones were transferred to Swinegate to operate on Kirkstall–Roundhay and Belle Isle in particular. They did not at first work much to Dewsbury Road, Half Mile Lane or on Meanwood–Elland Road and being without mechanical track brakes could not operate to Beeston. Nos. 501–520 finally operated from Swinegate, 501 being 2099 renumbered and retaining its London livery. These cars were generally popular in the city and although they tended to be rather noisy, especially on points and crossings, they gave a smooth ride on the sleeper track in York Road, much of which had been relaid and was in good condition. It was about this time that experience in laying the Gipton and Belle Isle extensions in concrete, rather than wooden sleepers and ballast, was applied to existing sleeper track routes by setting the rails in a continuous concrete bed and replacing the ballast. Long stretches were dealt with in 1952 on Princes Avenue and subsequently on the Middleton and York Road routes up to 1956.

Following the placing in service of 550, the GEC equipped 'Feltham' cars began to be dealt with and these were classified UCC/2, with numbers from 551. My recollection of them is that they were generally in poorer condition, rattled rather more internally, and the GEC contactor equipment was less reliable. I remember travelling from Whingate to City Square on No. 560 when the contactor cut out at notch six or seven going downhill. How the car behaved going uphill to Crossgates is better not imagined! These cars were placed in service in order up to 560 and then the better ones, 561/2/79/81/3/6/8/90 appeared between January and June 1952, while 563/4/5/6/70/80/9 were repolished internally and repainted externally, but not put into service, between January and March 1952.

Experiments were made early in 1951 with pantographs, used successfully in Sunderland and, of course, very extensively outside the United Kingdom for tramway purposes, in order to avoid the need for reversing the bow and reduce the risk of drivers running with it facing forward, which could be very damaging to the overhead equipment. 'Feltham' cars were used for the experiments, 517 being fitted in January 1951, and 528–30 in March. The experiments ended in a very unfortunate incident which was happily no more serious. Mr. Matterface described it at a public lecture he gave and the circumstances were that one of the cars fitted was out on a test run and was entering City Square when the curved end of the collector slide caught under one of the span wires and was catapulted on to the roof of the Majestic cinema. It was fortunate that it landed on the roof rather than among the pedestrians on the pavement. The incident was inevitable because the pantograph was centrally mounted whilst the overhead was aligned for a trailing bow collector which was effectively over the rear axle or bogie, and hence on curves the collector plate on the pantograph was not central on the overhead. The experiments were ended and the four cars fitted with standard bow collectors in June 1951. An alternative means of preventing drivers running with the bow collector reversed suggested after this was to paint sections of the bow collector rope red and green in such a way that when the bow was trailing the driver would see the green section and if it was facing he would see the red. This idea was not adopted but I believe odd cars were experimentally dealt with.

The placing in service of these sixty-nine cars permitted the withdrawal of many older cars and resulted in the final demise during 1951–2 of the remaining Hull cars, rebuilt balconies, with and without air brakes, the remaining Hamilton air braked cars built enclosed and all but two of the Hamilton bodied pivotal cars – 396 and 408 which had P.35 trucks as described earlier. A start was made on withdrawing Chamberlain pivotal trucked cars, both Leeds built and particularly the Brush/GEC ones, while two Manchester cars and five Southamptons were also withdrawn.

A further London car which came to Leeds at this time was the famous LCC No. 1, the Bluebird, which had an improved version of the typical London body. In Leeds it was not classified, although it could well have been F2, and was numbered 301. It entered service in the new lined red livery with a large area of cream above the lower saloon windows, similar to the 'Feltham' cars, and retained the side indicators under the stairs, being unique in Leeds in having four combined destination and number blinds. Internally it retained the royal blue and turquoise paint used in London, and was generally a comfortable car to ride in. Electrically, however, it was on a par with the HR2s, although having EMB interlocking air wheel brake equipment as well as magnetic track brakes, but like them its acceleration was not good, despite four motors, and it was not popular with the staff. It worked from Chapeltown depot until that depot was closed, and generally operated on the Roundhay–Moortown routes thereafter.

The final demise of the London Tramways was clearly in sight in late 1950 and there was still interest in transferring the 1930 built HR2s to other undertakings, Glasgow being particularly interested. The Chief Inspecting Officer at the Ministry of Transport would not sanction their operation on any other undertaking unless air brakes were fitted, so Leeds and Glasgow shared the cost of modifying one of the two remaining cars in Leeds still retaining only hand and magnetic track brakes. No. 278 was selected and re-entered service in February 1951 after being extensively modified by the fitting of an air wheel braking system similar to the 'Feltham' cars, operated by a standard Leeds style air valve, but retaining its magnetic track brake. It also had platform doors fitted, was re-upholstered, fitted with single blind indicators, buzzers and new bells, and then operated on a greater variety of routes, including some spells from Chapeltown on the Lawnswood–Moortown–Roundhay routes. It was one of the four cars experimentally painted in Kearsley's Post Office red during 1951. However, in view of the cost established in converting No. 278 the other Leeds car (279) remained as it was, and no other transfers were arranged.

The original Middleton bogie, No. 255, had not been operating on the Middleton route for some time prior to 1952, as it was not as fast at the later ones and it had worked not infrequently to Hunslet, and occasionally on other routes. It remained in the pre-1948 blue livery and, with Nos. 272–4 and ex London 279, was one of the few Leeds pre-Feltham cars which never had cream window frames. The need for high speed

**Plate 46** Ex-London 'Feltham' car No. 2158 as Leeds No. 581 in lined red livery at Whingate, 24 May 1952

*(Author)*

**Plate 47** Ex-London No. 1 as Leeds No. 301 in its first red livery at Roundhay 17 May 1952. Also shown are Horsfield No. 214 and streamliner No. 273

*(Author)*

cars was great and No. 255 was therefore modernised with new high speed motors and electro pneumatic equipment similar to the other cars, after which it resumed regular working on the Middleton service.

The original Southampton car (290) was given an overhaul in July 1951, being the only one so distinguished, during which the interior green paint was changed to medium brown, which was much pleasanter, and improved two-and-one better upholstered seating was provided. It was also equipped with a single blind indicator and repainted in standard red and cream with two cream bands, both lined, which again distinguished it from any others.

From 1950 problems had been experienced in obtaining spares for GEC equipped cars of all classes and a start was made in substituting controllers, and later motors, with various Metro-Vick and BTH types. The first cars dealt with were Brush/GEC Chamberlains (class B1/2) and Nos. 15 and 16 were fitted with BTH510H controllers, later a number of others being given OK9B, and in 1952 Nos. 28 and 29 were given MV114 motors also. Nos. 24 and 39, which already had MV114 motors also received OK9B controllers, and thus all these four cars finally became B1 although, as remarked upon earlier, no official recognition was ever made of these changes. The OK9B controllers very probably came from the Southampton cars which were not overhauled and placed in service, but later withdrawals of Leeds cars also provided a supply.

There was a considerable amount of lining out involved in applying the standard red livery, and although the brown indicator woodwork and ventilator windows had been replaced by red, further simplification was thought necessary, presumably because of mounting painting costs, so in June 1952 a further selection of experimental repaintings was done. Five cars (1, 36, 196, 219, 242) were painted unlined standard crimson with full black edging and the bands below the windows pale green. 219 had a black truck but the others had normal brown. Eight cars (70, 132, 146, 186, 253, 270, 272, 283) were painted unrelieved crimson, but with full black edging, three (29, 130 and 166) were standard unlined red with light jade or turquoise green bands, and two (28, 220) unlined red and cream. Out of all this selection the unlined version of the red and cream was adopted as standard, and all the green bands were quite soon over-painted with cream, but of the plain red cars only 132, 186 and 253 had the cream added, the others remaining plain until withdrawn or repainted, either of which had in all cases taken place by September 1953. This plain red and cream remained the standard livery, with only minor simplification, until the end of operations.

There was still at this time activity towards improving the efficiency and internal finish of the cars and outward signs of this were the already described modifications of Horsfield No. 179 and London HR2 278, and the internal refurbishing of No. 187 with plastic type panelling, very similar to that now usual on buses, and this car also was repolished with lighter woodwork. Additionally the long bench seats at the ends of the top deck were replaced with two single ones facing forward at the window side, which reduced seating capacity to fifty-six. The bench seat was later restored, but the panelling of course remained, the car lasting to the end. In the report for the year ended 31 March 1951, it was noted that experimental work was also being undertaken into the correlation between wheel gauge and track gauge, with resilient gear wheels and road wheels, and with springs, as well as interior finishes as described. So if the trams were to continue in operation, they were going to be kept as much up to date as possible.

An unhappily notable event on 4 September 1952 was a second accident which was the subject of a Ministry of Transport enquiry. The circumstances were that when former London 'Feltham' car No. 507 was being reversed at Roundhay Park, the driver left to call in the adjacent convenience and while he was away the car ran away. The air brake handle had to be in the 'neutral' position with reservoir and exhaust valves closed in order to be taken out, and the Inspecting officer concluded that the driver had held the car on a minimum pressure of air and, in removing the handle, had probably just opened the exhaust valve sufficiently that leakage would allow the car to move. Being prepared to change ends he had also removed the reverser from the controller, which had the effect of locking it in the 'off' position and had taken both with him, but had not applied the hand parking brake as regulations required before leaving the car. When the car began to move the conductor was only able to try to stop it with the hand parking brake, in which he was unsuccessful, and at the enquiry admitted to not knowing where the emergency air brake was. The Conductor Training Inspector agreed that conductors were not specifically shown the position of this valve, but were told where it was, as it was quite prominent outside the driver's cab, painted red, and marked 'Emergency Brake'. When the car was still running quite slowly onto the reservation below the Park, the conductor jumped off (see the Morley accident also), stating at the enquiry that he was sure the car would become derailed on the stretch of track at that time being altered from wooden sleepers to concrete bed (see page 108), and which at that time was not permanently fixed at all. Cars were passing over at drastically reduced speed, but the runaway passed over at an estimated speed of 40 mph, without mishap, and continued at increasing speed towards Oakwood, where at an estimated speed of 50 mph it negotiated the reverse curves without derailment and collided with English Electric Chamberlain No. 92, about to depart from the stop. The conductor of this car saw it approaching and shouted a warning to the passengers, he, and some on the platform having time to jump off. The violent impact sent No. 92 forward at equally high speed, unfortunately knocking the driver over, so that he struck his head on the bulkhead door behind him, and was unconscious. This car also negatiated two sharp curves and was finally stopped by a passenger between the Gipton Hotel and Ditchburns works. No. 507 left the rails and came to rest upright against the curb in front of the Oakwood parade of shops.

The ends of both cars were extensively damaged and neither was repaired, 92 being withdrawn at once, and 507 on 28 July 1953. No. 92 had only returned to service after a complete overhaul in May 1952 and was in excellent condition. Twelve passengers and three staff were injured and eight people were detained in hospital, it being very fortunate that no one was killed either directly or indirectly in this incident.

Brigadier Langley conducted the enquiry and under his direction stringent tests were made of the effectiveness of the various braking systems of the 'Feltham' cars, particularly the leakage from the air brake system with the control handle in 'neutral', and the hand brake as a holding and stopping device. The 'Feltham' tested (No. 515) was towed (or attempted to be) by a Leeds Horsfield car (No. 199), and with considerably less than a full pressure brake application was not readily moved, as shown in the following table.

*PULLING TESTS*

| Air in brake (lbs per sq in – max 90) | Controller notch reqd. on pulling car to *move* UCC car. |
|---|---|
| 10 | 1 |
| 40 | 3 |
| 80 | 4 pulling car slipping |
| Handbrake full on | 4 pulling car slipping |

*RUNNING TEST*

Without power car reached 20 mph in 83 yards. Handbrake stopped car in 65 yards from 20 mph. Brigadier Langley concluded that the brakes were thoroughly efficient.

The car was then allowed to run without power to Oakwood and reached 30 mph before the track repairs, over which it was taken at 10 mph and then easily reached 30 mph again before being braked for Oakwood.

It was concluded that the accident was attributable mainly to the driver not having applied the handbrake in the first place and somewhat less to the conductor. It was recommended that conductors should be shown specifically the emergency brake arrangements on all classes of car during their training.

Traffic in the city was rapidly increasing, however, as it was everywhere else, the trams ran through some of the less wide streets, and there were very few examples of one way working. Although power points were installed it was necessary to slow down approaching them and at places like the Briggate–Boar Lane cross roads, this slowed other traffic considerably. Tram tracks were always laid in the middle of the road and as the tramway authority was responsible for road maintenance between the rails and also 1ft 6in outside the outer rails in the formation, layouts were not likely to be devised in which the position of the rails suited 'lane' discipline with a consequent increase in the area of road surface to be maintained. Naturally trams making left turns at busy junctions broke all the principles of present day lane discipline by moving from the crown of the road to the left. Conductors were obliged to give hand signals from the rear platform, which was not satisfactory for vehicles alongside as the trams had no mechanical indicators. At many termini they stood in the middle of the road and although refuges had been provided at a number of places – for instance Harehills, Chapeltown, Haddon Place – and a number were in the central reservation at the ends of reserved track routes, there remained many places where they were an undesirable obstruction. Where cars used crossovers in the city area, such as Briggate, it became increasingly difficult to avoid congestion by traffic becoming blocked behind a tram which was about to reverse.

City Square was becoming another major problem. The track layout had been put in the centre area, with the queue barriers, in 1937, and this then had many advantages for passengers and other traffic, but as traffic grew, it began to cause considerable congestion. The routing of trams was such that those running to and from Park Row came from and went to Boar lane, whereas a considerable proportion of other traffic came from Wellington Street and Infirmary Street and crossed to Bishopsgate Street. Traffic jams quite often built up because traffic coming round the top of City Square obstructed trams leaving towards Park Row. This stopped other cars moving up to load, and a queue of cars reached back into Boar Lane, preventing traffic flowing into Bishopsgate Street. Such situations were only retrieved by judicious closing up of vehicles or trams. The complications at this junction were such that the trams had their own system of traffic signals.

It was now generally acknowledged that they caused congestion in the city centre, but the large lengths of reserved track in the suburbs and the greater permitted size of trams, which gave a carrying capacity advantage over most buses which still had a size limit to 27ft 6in length, and therefore were restricted to fifty-eight to sixty seats, with eight standing as against the trams twelve, seemed to justify consideration of ways to alleviate the city centre congestion with trams rather than replace them. A number of schemes were considered, involving alterations to the cross linking of routes to obviate as far as possible left turns in the central area – through working between Roundhay/Moortown

**Plate 48** Ex London No. 1881 as Leeds No. 277 after its eye-catching overhaul and repaint in 1948 at Roundhay 2 August 1948

*(Author)*

**Plate 49** The all electric railcar No. 602 on a press demonstration at Templenewsam, June 1953

*(Copyright Yorkshire Post Newspapers)*

and Belle Isle/Middleton was a major feature. Much of this principle has been built into the present bus routing system, although the one way street system has created problems, and there is probably more left-turning into Briggate than ever!

The tunnels idea naturally came to the fore again and once again the question of cars to operate in them was developed, two results following from this. The first was the decision to have two very modern single deckers built, with varying electrical equipment for comparison, and Messrs. C. H. Roe of Crossgates undertook this. One had conventional but very modern equipment with EMB lightweight resilient bogies, the other was all-electric with the VAMBAC (variable automatic multi notch braking and control) system of control and M & T inside bearing resilient bogies. The bodies were similar, with centre entrance/exit, with seventeen seats in each saloon, and were up to the best standards of bus body construction of the time. They were intended to carry up to thirty-two standing passengers (eight in each saloon, and sixteen in the centre vestibule) when necessary at the peaks. Both cars entered service on 1 June 1953, the more conventional one being 601 and the VAMBAC one 602, painted in a special royal purple and ivory livery with gold lining, to acknowledge their introduction in Coronation year.

They were tried on all routes and were very well received, particularly in that they demonstrated that a modern tram could have excellent performance characteristics and be very quiet in operation. The idea of many more passengers standing was not popular, however, as people in Leeds were not particularly impressed by what might be the case on London's tubes or on continental single deck tramcars. The wheel at first swung the other way so that 76–78 seat buses in Leeds were operated 'no standing'. More recently, under 'one-man operation', up to 18 standees are permitted. The cost of the new cars was about £12,000 for 601 and £13,000 for 602, very much more than a contemporary double deck bus.

The second result of the re-consideration of the tunnels scheme was the decision to press on with rebuilding the former Sunderland single decker but it still was not completed quickly and its entry to service was some time later than 601–2.

There was, needless to say, considerable objection to the retention of trams at all and the question inevitably became involved with local politics, the controlling Labour party being ranged on the abandonment front and the opposing Conservatives the retention. The question was made the main transport argument in local elections and as the Labour party remained in control of the council, abandonment was decided upon in 1953, to be spread over ten years. The Transport committee chairman made the announcement not long after he had taken official delivery of the two new single deckers and predicted their being the forerunners of a fleet of such cars to transform urban transport in the city. Abandonment was explained as being necessary for economic reasons and the plan was to replace those routes in the west of the city in order to clear City Square of trams as quickly as possible. This programme advantageously maintained most of the good reserved track routes until the later stages.

It is interesting to recall that in Liverpool the political parties were in reversed positions, but that the party in power supported abandonment while the opposition supported retention. The inference is clear, that the economic facts could not be overlooked and that trams could not be bought, operated and maintained profitably at the fares levels which could reasonably be charged. So far as Leeds was concerned quite a few facts are available which demonstrated the difficulties. The annual report of the Transport committee to the Council each year from 1947 included a comment about some item or other which was causing concern. I have already described how fare increases were made in 1945 and 1946 after twenty-two years of stability, but whereas after the first world war a serious depression set in and, unhappily for those who suffered, created a situation where wage reductions could be enforced, and fares reduced, no such situation developed after 1945. Some interesting comments were made in 1948 about the price of rails at £25.15s.10d. per ton against £11.19s.0d. pre-war and at the same time it was noted that bus operating costs (diesel oil, licences, etc.) were not rising like tramway costs for rails, electrical energy, trolley wire cable etc. Deficits on the total operation continued to be reported and in 1951 a further Public Enquiry was held to consider a proposed fare increase. This same year a wage award was reported as costing £38,000 per annum, while in 1948 the annual payroll exceeded £1 million and in 1952 wages accounted for 11s.10½d. in every £1 of expenditure. A reduction in traffic was reported for the third year in succession, and to compensate tramcar mileage was reduced in two years by 1,032,027 without any route withdrawals taking place, although late Saturday cars ran till 11.30 pm. The reduction was achieved by cutting out short workings, made possible by the continuing movement of population away from the former densely populated areas, and reducing frequencies as a result of the general reduction in traffic already described. Specific timetable changes about this time were the reduction of Hyde Park–Belle Isle workings to peak hours only and Saturdays excepted from 18 August 1952, of Swinegate–Beeston workings to Saturdays excepted and withdrawal of Harehills–Beeston workings after 6.20 pm Monday to Saturday and altogether on Sundays. Other areas of economy were explored and £60,000 was saved, but the deficit for the year ended 31 March 1954, for the whole undertaking, was £64,392.

The fleet now contained only four cars less than seventeen years old, so that replacement of about half was really necessary within the next few years and the remainder within the decade. At this time a new tram (assuming a contractor could be found to build it) was costing about three times the price of a new bus and had considerable disadvantages, not least of which could be said to be its longevity which caused operators to have obsolescent cars running because they were too good to scrap. The decision to abandon was inevitable and history has shown that, except for the very specialised Promenade route in Blackpool and its inter-urban continuation to Fleetwood, every other British undertaking and very many others, with or without political intervention, was forced to the same conclusion, in some cases involving the disposal for scrap of modern post-war tramcars which had by no means become obsolete – notably Glasgow, Sheffield, Aberdeen and Edinburgh.

**Plate 50** Horsfield car No. 179 after modernisation with uniquely placed single blind indicators, Pullman ventilators and resilient wheeled EMB flexible axle truck. Photographed at Middleton 12 May 1952 in lined red livery

*(Author)*

CHAPTER 8

# Decline and termination

The abandonment policy was implemented within the year, when buses replaced the 14 tram service from Corn Exchange to Half Mile Lane, Stanningley from 4 October 1953. The replacement buses were forty-six older ones which were re-licenced for this and other extensions, and they worked from the Central bus station via Eastgate and Vicar Lane, which left the Corn Exchange turning circle for the exclusive use of West Riding buses from Rothwell and Wakefield. Although for many years the Stanningley route had been exclusively worked by Horsfield air cars, provided by Bramley until its closure in 1949, and generally provided by Swinegate after that, there was no real reason for such cars to be used, and increasing use had been made of other P.35 trucked cars, including Manchesters, but, as stressed by other writers, not Pivotals, nor Felthams, nor Hulls.

During 1953 there had been a steady withdrawal of cars, but after the withdrawal of the Half Mile Lane service twenty-five were withdrawn at once, which left only seventeen pivotal cars and three Manchesters in service, and saw the last Southamptons withdrawn. Among the cars withdrawn were the last blue ones and these included examples in all the liveries since 1947, Nos. 98, 435/43 being in the cream banded livery with unlined top deck panels, Nos. 5 and 61 in dark blue with cream indicator woodwork, Nos. 75, 431/6/8 in dark blue with brown indicator woodwork, Nos. 19, 26, 42/5, 421/7/8/41/2/5 in standard Royal blue and No. 69 in the special blue livery with blue window frames used on three cars in 1950–1. The last car to run in the post war standard livery with lined top deck panels was No. 27, painted on 3 June 1945 and withdrawn on 7 November 1952, looking rather scruffy! A number of other blue cars remained until early in 1953, but these were then repainted, although the pivotal trucked ones among them were withdrawn by 3 April 1954.

The next abandonment followed on 3 April 1954 when the Kirkstall Abbey and Compton Road trams were replaced by a new No. 4 bus service running through the city via the Headrow. Previously Kirkstall

Road trams had worked through to Harehills and Roundhay, as they had started to do in 1897, and the Compton Road trams had worked to Dewsbury Road. To balance the workings, through operation was commenced between Roundhay or Harehills and Dewsbury Road, a new connection between Briggate and Lower Briggate having been provided in the south bound direction to permit this. Previously the only cars running from Briggate to Lower Briggate had been those going to the depot, and they had had to work via the Corn Exchange, a sharp curve existing from Briggate to Duncan Street which lacked an auto point changer. Cars using this had to have the conductor stand in front with the hand point rod, wait until the car had passed to restore the points, and then run round the corner after it. This usually caused inconvenience to other traffic, the traffic lights often changing while the manoeuvre was going on.

The reduction in the tram fleet already effected and contemplated allowed the closure of Headingley depot to trams to be accomplished simultaneously and it was devoted entirely to buses. Seventeen cars were withdrawn on 3 April 1954, and these included the remaining pivotal cars and the remaining Manchesters. Odd cars continued to be withdrawn when not considered to justify repair and before the next major route abandonment two GEC Horsfields (241/5), the second 1935 streamliner, four P.35 Chamberlains and the remaining 1928 Hamilton style car on a P.35 truck had been withdrawn.

The placing in service of cars was not at an end despite all these withdrawals and on 4 August 1954 the rebuilt Sunderland single decker took the road, the only resemblance with its former state being the side windows to the saloons. Otherwise it followed as far as practicable the design of the Roe built cars, although it did not have the same elegance of line and easy curves. It was in the standard red with cream window frames and a large shaped cream painted sheet along the side of the roof to obscure the equipment mounted on the roof, which was otherwise painted pale grey. A new centre entrance was provided and EMB Heavyweight 'Johannesburg' bogies replaced the HR/2 type bogies which Leeds had acquired for it. It was provided with electro pneumatic control equipment similar to No. 601, air wheel and magnetic track brakes, and WT 84 motors, with 71:14 gearing and twenty-seven inch wheels. It was put to work on the Hunslet route, along with the other two single deckers, as the three of them could maintain the service for most of the day. Thus this short street route in the most industrial part of the city had the most modern cars in the fleet, and they were, of course, completely inhibited and unable to realise their potential speed and acceleration.

The short Gipton Estate route was taken over by buses from 24 April 1955, the buses running to and from Vicar Lane only, making a small circle in the central area. The trams had worked through from

Dewsbury Road, and these now worked to Chapeltown and Moortown, which reduced turning in Briggate, as not all these cars had come through from the Lawnswood service in the past. Although there was no immediate withdrawal of cars as a result of this, Chapeltown depot was closed and used for storing surplus cars for a time, until it was modified as the Corporation's Central Purchasing Depot. It still exists, further rebuilt as Technorth's premises.

During the early part of 1955 some interesting innovations were made to GEC equipped cars which were needed for a little longer. As mentioned earlier spares were becoming difficult to find, particularly for controllers, and those of the GEC Horsfields and Felthams were becoming a problem. Twenty-two GEC Felthams had not yet been placed in service, although seven of these had been refurbished and repainted. The first move was the fitting of MV OK9B controllers to Horsfield No. 253 in December 1954, this car becoming the first in Leeds to have such a controller with an integral air track brake valve. No. 214 was soon after altered, and also received fresh motors, which sounded like MV 101. Subsequently Nos. 229/52 received fresh controllers and motors, 209/13 fresh motors and 246 fresh controllers. The performance of these cars with new controllers was much improved, particularly smoothness of starting, as the controller steps had suffered from wear, thus making smooth acceleration impossible. I recall No. 206 about this time on which in series no power reached the motors until notch three out of four which resulted in violent starting and all power was lost on notch five, the transfer from series to parallel, which also resulted in a severe surge when the next notch was reached. Cars in this condition added to the evidence that the sooner they finally disappeared the better.

Two of the repainted and stored Feltham cars (570/80) were placed in service in February 1955, followed in March by Nos. 563–6/89, 563 being equipped with OK9B controllers instead of the GEC contactor type. All these entered service in the old fully lined livery and it was pleasant to see newly painted cars in this style again. Three more (567/9/87) were fully repolished internally and repainted externally in the unlined livery, No. 587 having OK9B controllers, and the whole of this class in service was then quickly fitted with them, their performance becoming much more reliable. For a time one of the Metro-Vick cars (530) ran so equipped but later had its OK33B controllers restored. The success of this led to the placing in service of five more of the stored cars between April and July 1956 (in order of appearance 568/73/85/74/82) all equipped with OK9B controllers from the start and repainted but not repolished inside, so that they retained the dark oak wood. No. 585 had an M & T motormans air brake valve as well. The remaining seven cars were burned for scrap between 5 July and 9 November 1956.

Overhaul and repainting of cars for use during the final stages continued but a surprising event during July 1955 was the external repainting of Chamberlain cars 60, 74/6, 84, 93, 124/39, which, in the event, lasted no longer than eleven of their fellows not so distinguished. All these cars had much less black at this repainting and were in very good condition. In general the first six months of 1955 were very interesting ones indeed for the observer.

So far as other people were concerned (and that meant the great majority) the trams were now regarded as out of date and the time had been reached when they began to have a serious effect on traffic where even in moderately busy roads problems were arising at tram stops where passengers had to walk into the road. The revision of routes following the closures so far effected had cut out some of the city centre turns which caused problems but much of the system still remained, and lines of cars were still a feature of busy roads like Briggate, Boar Lane, Duncan Street and on Leeds Bridge, in City Square and at the Corn Exchange. Tunnels and so forth were now decidedly ruled out and the ten year plan had been accelerated to an estimated final abandonment in 1960.

A major through route withdrawal accompanied by some considerable associated bus route revisions took place from 26 June 1955 when the Meanwood–City–Elland Road cars were displaced. The Morley buses already ran along Elland Road, having replaced trams on 22 January 1935, and these were extended from the Corn Exchange to a new terminus at Meanwood where they did not obstruct other traffic as the trams had done, both Meanwood and Elland Road tram termini being road centre ones. In addition a new service was introduced between Meanwood and Cottingley Estate, numbered 8, and the former bus services 29 City Square–Cottingley and 48 Beeston–Middleton were merged to give a new 29 service City Square–Beeston–Middleton. This generally gave improved services in the areas affected. The tracks to Elland Road remained for a little while to give access to the tramcar graveyard along Low Fields Road siding. Quite soon, however, cars were taken there by low-loader.

Thirty-four cars were taken out of service the next day and this, surprisingly to the observer at the time, included nineteen GEC Horsfields. I have described how earlier in the year a number of these were equipped with fresh motors and controllers but the general condition of these must clearly have been such that it was a better proposition to keep Chamberlain cars which were still in satisfactory condition running a little longer. Seventeen of the twenty-nine GEC Horsfields remaining, however, lasted until 29 March 1959.

The Beeston trams were replaced by buses from 21 November 1955, the only alteration being that through working to Harehills was discontinued altogether and pre-war AEC/Roe buses 106–25 were repainted and used for this in the first stage. Eighteen Chamberlain cars were withdrawn after this, including Nos. 34/8 which were the last small wheeled P.35 retrucks. Torre Road depot was closed to trams from this date also and all the remaining cars operated from Swinegate, Torre Road being modified to deal only with buses and being able to accommodate 230 after the alterations.

The Lawnswood route soon followed on 4 March 1956, releasing another twenty-five cars, all Chamberlains, for withdrawal. The replacement bus service was linked with the Beeston service, operating via Bishopsgate Street and Neville Street and its introduction was followed by loud protests from users that they could not travel to the places in the city to which they had always gone – i.e. they were taken to City Square instead of the Corn Exchange. At the same time, of course, passengers from Roundhay and Moortown were unable to ride through to City Square and the University and this also provoked vociferous complaint. This serves, I feel, to demonstrate that people become accustomed to behaving in certain ways and resent any change. It is certainly the case that as many people now travel through Briggate on the buses as travelled through Briggate on trams, so that the change has probably been beneficial to a number as great as that to which it has been detrimental.

Although a large batch of cars was withdrawn after each abandonment, they continued to be taken out of service if they needed expensive repair work in between and this applied particularly to the Middleton bogie cars, the first of which were withdrawn on 17 February 1956 (Nos. 255/67) the remainder going as they required attention up to 27 January 1957, but No. 268 survived until 28 September 1957.

This left only the Whingate and New Inn trams running through City Square and they were replaced from 22 July 1956, some extensive service changes being made as a consequence. The new through service to Whingate was provided by an extension of the Bus Station–Seacroft services (78 and 79) which took over the numbers 15 and 16, running via Kirkgate and City Square as the trams had done. The new service to New Inn was provided by a similar extension of the Gipton buses, the terminus at New Inn being dispensed with and a new one at Greenthorpe brought into use. This at first brought the Crossley buses 701–21 into the city centre regularly for the first time but they were soon transferred to other routes operated from the newly opened Seacroft garage. The tram workings were altered so that the York Road cars ran to Belle Isle and Middleton, cars working Halton–City–Belle Isle–Middleton–City–Crossgates and reverse, with Templenewsam cars starting in Kirkgate as previously, plus certain short workings to Belle Isle and Harehills Lane. A crossover was put in at the Central bus station and this was a new destination added to the blinds of certain cars. It was normally used by cars from Belle Isle, although never very frequently.

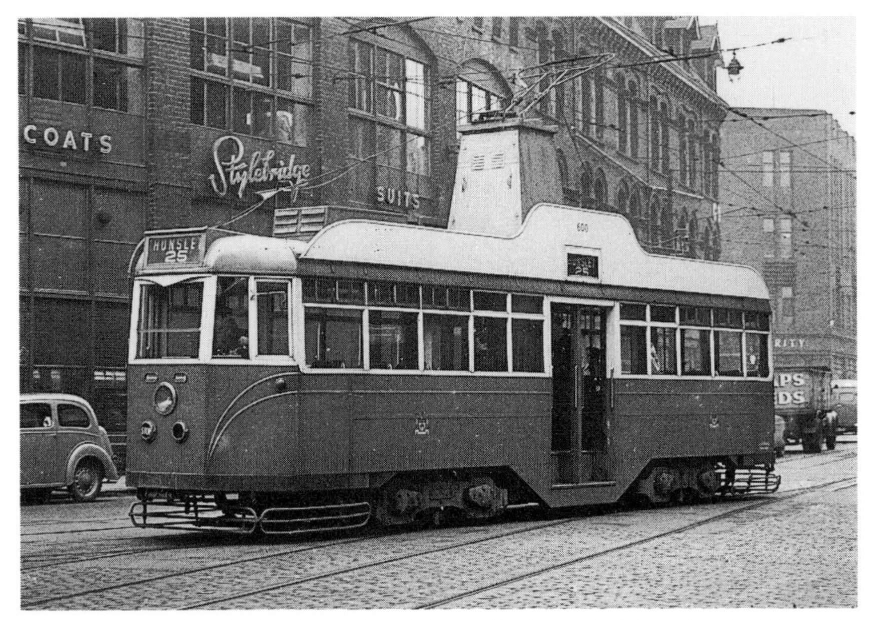


**Plate 51** Ex-Sunderland car No. 85, as finally rebuilt as Leeds No. 600, entering Swinegate

*(Copyright Leeds City Transport)*

**Plate 52** The last day of operation, 7 Nov 1959 and Horsfield No. 187 waits for departure to Crossgates

*(Copyright Yorkshire Post Newspapers)*

The Middleton–Belle Isle circle had, with assistance from Horsfield cars, especially after circular working started in 1949, been the preserve of the Middleton bogie cars but the number of cars involved in the new workings was clearly far greater than the eight which remained, and Horsfields and Felthams were obviously going to bear the brunt of the working. The remaining high speed cars did appear in the city centre, where they had not been seen regularly since the Middleton, Belle Isle and Hunslet cars finally had their terminus moved to Swinegate on 20 October 1939 after experiments during the previous three Christmases, and along York Road, but after January 1957 only 268 remained and it continued to operate on these workings until the withdrawal of all the remaining non-standard cars on 28 September 1957, described later. The Horsfield and Feltham cars, the latter fitted with back sanding equipment as a guard against running back, performed adequately enough on the Middleton circle, but there was no longer the exciting surge of a Middleton bogie on full power up through the woods. The cars withdrawn after 22 July 1956 were all the remaining eighteen Chamberlain cars, a number of which had been stored for a while after 4 March and were reinstated whilst the Felthams were modified, and the first three GEC Felthams (552/5/79). Of the Chamberlains Nos. 60 and 74 were in particularly good condition when withdrawn and it seemed a pity that the half dozen best Chamberlains could not have been retained in preference to some very run down GEC Horsfields and Felthams which were. No doubt eliminating hand brake only cars was a major – and justifiable – attraction.

This withdrawal completed the first phase of removing trams from Boar Lane, City Square and Wellington Street but for the moment track from Swinegate, up Bishopsgate Street, through City Square and along Wellington Street into Kirkstall Road had to be retained to ferry cars to and from works. This finally ceased from 8 November 1957 when facilities for all the work necessary to non-removable parts of the cars were moved from Kirkstall Road to Swinegate, which then became a combined running shed and workshop as Kirkstall Road had been in its earliest days. Kirkstall Road was then modified for use as the central bus repair shop. Until this happened no real progress could be made with the re-designing of City Square and one or two efforts were made before it attained its present appearance. It is hard indeed to imagine days when traffic moved in both directions round all its sides, with trams moving into and out of the central area.

The next route scheduled for abandonment was Moortown–City–Dewsbury Road and the buses for this had been ordered. Before the closure could be implemented, however, the Suez affair occurred with its threat to oil supplies. To achieve immediate economies the times of all last buses were brought forward and the transport committee issued a statement that no further tramway abandonment would take place until the position, in particular concerning oil supplies, was very much clearer. The Elland Road route was still intact and tramcar football specials were reintroduced on 8 December 1956. The second 'last car' ran on 16 March 1957.

An immediate effect concerned certain GEC Horsfield cars which were being run down against the original date of this abandonment. Their condition was such that they could not be expected to continue running until a now uncertain date, so a number of them were given minor overhauls and externally repainted and this included all but No. 246 of those with modified equipment. The cars dealt with were Nos. 166, 205/9/13–6/22/9/40/7/52–4, and except for 205 all these survived until 28 March 1959.

The period of difficulty did not last long in the event and the Moortown–City–Dewsbury Road trams were replaced by buses from 29 September 1957. These tram workings had formed part of the Moortown–Roundhay circular workings and to maintain the essential part of this the new No. 2 bus service ran from Dewsbury Road to Roundhay Park via Moortown while the Roundhay Road trams ran to Moortown corner, thus giving a through service between Harehills and Moortown and Roundhay and Chapeltown and Dewsbury Road, as well as services to the city in both directions along Street Lane. The new bus service operated via Vicar Lane in both directions, as the centre queue barriers in Briggate could not be used for buses and the provision of bus stops on the pavement in addition would have been quite impossible in consideration of other traffic. Of course Street Lane passengers had a 'lucky dip' choice whether to wait in Briggate for a tram or Vicar Lane for a bus!

Twenty-eight cars were withdrawn at once and apart from the last Middleton bogie already noted these included all the remaining cars other than Horsfields and Felthams. Thus the 1943 Austerity car, the post war double decker, the two remaining London HR2s, the former London Bluebird and the three single deckers, as well as twelve BTH and seven GEC Felthams, were taken out of traffic. The only class now remaining intact was the BTH Horsfield, Nos. 155–204, but the first of these (189) was withdrawn on 4 November 1957, after an accident. The stored No. 180, now preserved in working order at Crich, was repaired instead, given the number 189, restored to service and ran until the end of operation.

Quite suddenly most of the interest had gone and the system could be seen to be decaying, although except for Half Mile Lane all the routes with major lengths of reservation remained in use, and BTH/Feltham and BTH/Horsfield cars were still being overhauled, the latter fitted with single blind indicators, and repainted externally. These, naturally enough, proved to be the cars which remained to the end.

No route withdrawals took place during 1958, but seventeen cars were withdrawn and the last cars to be fully repainted externally were dealt with during July. It cannot have been mere chance these were two of the experimental Leeds built Horsfield cars of 1930, No. 153 with GEC equipment and an EMB flexible axle truck of the type extensively used by Dundee and No. 154 with standard BTH equipment. Both were withdrawn on 29 March 1959, although 153 was working on Service 3 on the last evening, the driver remarking that 'it was taking some pushing along'. The shade of red used for these repaintings was noticeably brighter than had been standard, and one wondered if some extra white lead had been added to make it go further in the way in which the Caledonian Railway engines are reputed to have progressed from royal to sky blue in the early years of the century.

November 1958 saw the introduction on the Lawnswood–Beeston bus service of the first thirty foot long seventy-one seat bus, No. 221, after exhibition at the Commercial Motor Show. Early in 1959 the similar No. 245 began daily trial running round the Middleton and Moortown circular routes and the stage was set for the final abandonments during the year.

An odd way in which tramcar withdrawals caused difficulties in the city concerned prams. Through having a large platform at each end, sufficient space was available on trams for the very large, canopied, non-folding type of pram to be conveyed on the front platform, and many mothers took their babies to the city with them in such vehicles. As traffic increased it was bad enough to have passengers walking into the middle of the road to board the car at the rear, but when the driver and the mother started to load a large pram, sometimes still with the baby in it, on to the front platform, and it was a high lift on many cars, the road was very nearly blocked in both directions. The pram was then secured by a strap used to barricade the front platform when it was too warm to have the saloon door closed. Where cars loaded at the front in Briggate, cars with prams on, and the loading of the prams, caused all kinds of difficulties, including taking the pram off and putting it back again, and also rear loading, which caused the passengers to walk behind the car and stop the traffic, as the road was quite narrow and other traffic could only just pass the cars loading at the centre barrier. But the main advantage was really that the prams themselves could no longer be brought into the city, the pavements are thereby less obstructed and the problems which would undoubtedly have arisen in wheeling such large carriages across the present one way streets do not have to be faced by mothers or road users. I think for this we can probably be thankful.

The major abandonment took place on 29 March 1959, when the Belle Isle–Middleton circular service and Roundhay–Moortown were replaced by buses. A completely new group of bus services was introduced which basically provided through working between Dewsbury Road and Moortown–Roundhay–Belle Isle–Middleton–City and reverse, and also short workings between Belle Isle and Roundhay Park, and Dewsbury

Road and Moortown corner. Alternate buses to Middleton via Dewsbury Road and Belle Isle ran to a new terminus at Thorpe Lane, the others performing the circular workings. Middleton buses via Dewsbury Road ran under limited stop conditions during the peak periods to compensate for the rather longer journey time, as the route via Dewsbury Road and the Ring Road was longer. To cover the Moor Road section of the Middleton right of way, bus service No. 74 ran all day and was joined with No. 75 City Square to Beckett's Park to give a through service between Belle Isle and Beckett's Park throughout the day. The use of route No. 75 was discontinued. Seventy new seventy-one seat buses were brought into service to make this changeover, by far the largest single operation in the programme, and fifty-five trams were withdrawn, being all the remaining GEC Horsfields, all but one of the GEC Felthams, the remaining two Leeds built Horsfields, twenty BTH Horsfields and fifteen more BTH Felthams. This left twenty-eight BTH Horsfields and nineteen BTH Felthams to operate the remaining routes from Kirkgate to Crossgates, Templenewsam and Halton.

These changes did not include the short Hunslet route, but this followed on 19 April 1959 when a through bus route was introduced between North Lane and Hunslet via City Square and Lower Briggate, which incorporated the former 76 bus service. No trams were withdrawn at this point, although some of those retained did not do much work.

This situation continued until 7 November 1959 when buses gradually took over the existing tram duties after the 4.39 pm to Crossgates (Car No. 181), and the final rites were a procession of five cars each to Crossgates and Halton some two hours later, the first and last being illuminated. All ten were Horsfields, Nos. 178/2/1/98/1 to Crossgates, No. 178 being illuminated, and Nos. 173/6/89/75/60 to Halton, No. 160 being illuminated. The illuminated Crossgates car was the last one on the return, and was thus the last car to run in Leeds, being driven by Motorman Aisthorpe and the Transport committee chairman and Lady Mayoress. Considerable crowds gathered to hear the familiar rumbling for the last time and after the depot doors were closed for the last time a Civic banquet was held to mark the occasion.

The following day new bus routes were established between Horsforth and Crossgates, instead of Compton Road, and between Half Mile Lane and Halton. The Compton Road service was covered by diversion of the Horsforth (Stanhope Drive) and Bramley via Sandford routes from the Central bus station. Templenewsam was served from the Central bus station and some extensive road works had to be undertaken to permit the buses to reach a suitable terminus near the House.

A number of cars were bought or put aside for preservation, as described by J. Joyce in 'Tramway Twilight' and J. H. Price in the Veteran and Vintage series 'Tramcars' both published by Ian Allen, and most of those remaining are now at the National Tramway Museum at Crich in Derbyshire where an operational tramway exists. Others, I know, suffered from vandalism as a result of being in the open in an industrial area and had to be sold for scrap while something still remained. This unhappily included single decker No. 601. London No. 1 and Feltham No. 501 eventually returned to static display in that city.

During the latter years of the trams an extensive programme of sodium street lighting had been undertaken and on many tram routes alternate poles had been used for this by the addition of a cantilever bracket. This was done along Street Lane after the trams had been withdrawn. When closures took place the overhead was in general removed very quickly and the surplus poles were felled, but large numbers remain, including those along central reservations which had side poles and span wires. During the summer of 1979, for instance, those in Harrogate Road were repainted ready for a further spell of service.

Finances of the whole undertaking during the period of tramway decline had fluctuated, as fare increases were made in attempts to catch up with expenses with comment from time to time upon major problem areas. Fare increases were requested in 1954 to cover increased costs estimated at £321,600 per annum of which £271,600 was for wages while in 1957 an enquiry into a fare application to raise revenue to offset increased costs of £465,370 per annum was adjourned because agreement could not be reached on there not being a threepenny fare. Rising costs caused a five per cent reduction to be made in bus mileage, and whereas in 1952–3 a high turnover of staff was reported which was providing adequate staff numbers, by 1957 a severe staff shortage was reported, especially of platform staff. A wage award in 1957 was reported to be costing £123,578 per annum, and an application for a new fare structure calculated to raise £100,000 was granted. Total revenue exceeded £3 million in 1958–9, with passenger journeys at 205,484,462 and surpluses made in the years ending 31 March 1956, 1958, 1959 and 1960 wiped out the accumulated deficit, so when the trams finally went, the department had a surplus of £8,764 and it was reported that the drop in passengers had been stopped. It is probably not by chance that the deficit/surplus figures are generally inversely proportional to the tramcar mileage being operated.

There was mention in the 1958–9 report of the changeover causing some redundancy and certainly a number of older tram drivers never became bus drivers, although very many did. Many of the surplus tram men put in very useful service controlling the queues at the new bus stop in Briggate and other places until they retired and a number of tram drivers were retained over retiring age to keep driver training down to the minimum. For some time before withdrawal all additional workings to Roundhay Park had been covered by buses and there were a number of instances of buses working evening tramcar duties between Briggate and Moortown via Roundhay, which caused people seeing a bus to enquire 'is this a tram?' They did not at this time have suitable destination and number blinds for such circumstances and the situation was therefore confusing.

After each withdrawal the redundant street tracks were generally fairly quickly covered with tar and chippings leaving a very bad road surface as the tramway maintained section was often uneven and patching over the rails made it worse. It should be pointed out that the Transport department did not modernise its road maintenance equipment in the latter years when it could clearly be seen all responsibilities in this area would be lost and in consequence the old fashioned methods prevailed to the end, asphalt being shovelled, raked and rolled. This did not give an even surface by comparison with the modern machine methods. Such equipment was used to cover the tracks in certain later stages – Street Lane was an example – and at a later date the Highways department resurfaced their portion to give a new surface overall. On the reservations the rails and sleepers were quickly lifted and eventually the land itself was tidied up. Different treatments were used, the Stanningley Road length being planted with bushes, the soil being surrounded by stone walls, although it had been derelict for a number of years after being abandoned in October 1953. Most of the rest was sown with grass, but the original length from Harehills to Oakwood was not dealt with for many years.

In certain streets, particularly in the city, the track was lifted before the road was remade and I recall that in Park Row the whole of the tramways maintained portion of the road was made of granite blocks, with all sides flat, as distinct from the more typical cobble stones, and these proved extremely difficult to lift up. A pneumatic drill simply made a hole without disturbing the blocks to any useful extent. All the main roads involved were eventually completely resurfaced by machine, in most cases followed by a raising of the kerbstones and remaking of the footpaths. As a consequence bus travel became smoother than one would have considered possible in, say, 1956, but, just as poor track maintenance caused rough riding by tram, so does poor road maintenance cause rough riding by bus, too common in 1990–91.

Tram track is still buried under many roads and various excavations from time to time reveal it, often causing difficulties for the job in hand. The last visible track at Easterly Road bottom and Oakwood was removed during the Summer of 1972, so that, apart from the overhead poles now used for street lighting, little trace remains of the eighty-nine years of rail-borne public transport vehicles in the city.

An interesting point, perhaps, is that the presence of trams in York Road was from time to time given as the reason for not proceeding with the dual-carriageway extension from the Woodpecker Inn crossroads to

**Plate 53** The last two ceremonial cars from Crossgates and Templenewsam, with their drivers, in Swinegate Depot, 7 Nov 1959

*(Copyright Yorkshire Post Newspapers)*

**Plate 54** The ignominious end of many tramcars, fire. Hamilton balconies Nos 314 and 329 at Low Fields Road 25 Oct 1945

*(Copyright Yorkshire Post Newspapers)*

Lupton Avenue. A decade passed after their withdrawal before a start was made and the scheme finally completed includes a bridge at the Woodpecker Junction giving unimpeded access to York Road from the new Inner Ringroad Motorway. It has taken until 1990 to see work started on the second part of the bridge to give flyover access from York Road to the Ring Road.

In their later days, undoubtedly, the trams became scapegoats for much that was bad in the city traffic system, although I often wonder what might have been done with tram layouts in the light of present lane practise, one-way street systems and parking regulations. It would have been practicable today to have tram tracks alongside the kerb and, if appropriate, more than one track to allow trams to maintain lanes or even overtake, and a different situation might well have existed allied to dual carriageway reservations in the suburbs. However, such developments came at least a quarter of a century too late to permit useful retention of the excellent infrastructure which existed in south and east Leeds and could have been provided elsewhere. Mention of trams and one-way street system always bring to mind Birmingham's Alum Rock, Washwood Heath, Witton and Perry Barr cars proceeding along Corporation Street against the traffic flow, because impending withdrawal made the expense of diverting them quite unjustifiable. The result was one of the most unfortunate examples of trams not appearing adaptable to modern conditions.

So 'first generation' tramcars finally passed from Leeds, but after more than three decades many people still recall them with nostalgia and any display of models or photographs evokes great interest. Future generations will probably regard them as curiosities rather as we would regard a stage coach, but for many the memory is green. They served us very well in their heyday, they made possible the development of our cities and large towns to their present form in a way no other contemporary form of transport could have done and pointed the way to the present standards of urban development. Like railway steam engines they engendered ardent enthusiasts and diehard opponents, but in every town and city at their demise they had the goodwill of the crowds who turned out, recognising the end of an era. The tram we knew gave way for better things, its going facilitated many consequential improvements, but with it also disappeared something of the grace of more leisurely days which the urban dweller can perhaps ill afford to lose.

APPENDIX A

# Electric car liveries

A large variety of liveries has been mentioned in the preceding chapters and this was a major feature of interest, especially from 1948 onwards. Over the sixty-seven years of Corporation electric operation three principal changes of colour took place and these are worthy of detailed description, my own personal records covering the very interesting period from the end of the Second World War.

The first electric cars and trailers purchased by the Corporation in 1897 were painted in a blue and ivory livery, the blue being used for the dash and side panels, which were lined in gold and white, whilst the rocker panel was lined in either blue or black. The coat of arms was placed on the side of the waist panel, with the fleet number on either side of it, as well as on the dashes, with 'Leeds City Tramways' on the rocker panel. These original cars had 'Roundhay and Kirkstall' painted above the lower saloon windows.

The first change of colour took place with the introduction of the Dick Kerr cars in 1901, these being painted in yellow and white. The 1902 cars from Brush were painted in a modified version of this style with a chocolate dash, which became Mr. Hamilton's standard and basically remained unchanged until 1925. Details were as follows:

| | | |
|---|---|---|
| Dash panel | : | Chocolate brown edged in black and double lined in gold and white with square corners. When vestibules were added after 1910 these also were painted chocolate, the frames being lined in white and the panels above the windows in gold. The very large numbers were used after about 1903. |
| Rocker panel | : | White edged in black and lined in dark brown and (inside line) red, with square corners. |
| Lower saloon side panels | : | Primrose yellow edged in black and lined in gold and (inside line) red. At first the corners were very fancy scrolls and the number appeared twice. The coat of arms was placed in the centre with the lining out surrounding it. After 1910 square corners replaced the fancy ones and the side numbers disappeared. |

| | | |
|---|---|---|
| Upper deck saloon panels | : | Primrose yellow edged in black and lined in dark brown with curved corners. The lining was broken at the bulkhead on some cars and halfway between the end and the bulkhead on others. This inconsistency was perpetuated on the 1926 cars. Old photographs suggest that this may have arisen in the first place on account of the length of the side advertisements at first used. |
| All saloon window frames | : | White with brown drop windows, fan light ventilators where provided and indicator boxes. The curved areas on the bulkhead sides were scarlet lined in gold. |

This livery was recreated in 1948 when car No. 328 was restored as No. 309, although this included the very fancy corners on the lower deck side panels but not the side numbers and to this extent was not typical. The dash panels and vestibules were painted maroon on this occasion, the truck standard brown lined in white, and the roof black. The car ran with a bow collector. As I never saw the original livery, I cannot say whether the 'chocolate brown' referred to was really a dark maroon colour. The shade of yellow was deepened somewhat in 1925, but a major change was inaugurated in December that year by the new General Manager with the first of his new cars, No. 400.

The principal colours were blue and cream, the disposition and other details being as follows:

| | | |
|---|---|---|
| Dash panels | : | Dark blue edged in black lined in gold and (inside line) white with square corners. Smaller less ornate numbers were introduced. |
| Rocker panels | : | Cream edged in black and lined in black and dark blue (inside line) with square corners. |
| Lower saloon side panels | : | Dark blue edged in black lined in gold and (inside line) white with square corners. The coat of arms appeared in the centre, with the lining above and below at first, but later framing it in a circle. |
| Top deck panels | : | Cream lined in blue with rounded corners, the advertisement area and that above separately, and broken halfway between the bulkhead and the end. The inconsistency in this which had existed with the old cars continued with the new cars which followed, the Brush cars being like No. 400, but the English Electric and Leeds built cars had the lining broken at the bulkhead. These variations continued until the lining was discontinued after 1947. |
| Window frames and vestibules | : | Cream with brown indicator box woodwork and fan lights. Some cars had very thin blue lining on the vestibule struts. |
| Trucks and lifeguards | : | Dark maroon. |
| Roof | : | Grey. |

The next change was introduced with the Horsfield cars in 1930 when that part of the upper saloon panels used for advertisements was painted blue, lined in gold. These cars had this lining unbroken. Later some cars of all types had pale blue lining on the top deck panels and as the Horsfield cars had straight sides, the rocker panels disappeared. A deep cream band was introduced below the lower saloon windows on these cars, edged in black and lined in blue with the fleet number in large figures at the ends and small ones on the sides. When the balcony cars were enclosed, these ideas were followed up, the rocker panels being painted dark blue, lined in pale blue and a narrow cream band below the windows was added, while after about 1937 the entire top deck panelling was dark blue and the lining was straight as on the Horsfields. Later still the side and rocker panels were lined as an entity in gold. The remaining balcony cars also had all the top deck panels painted blue when they were repainted, and the last ones repainted blue had blue rocker panels separately lined out in blue.

After Mr. Vane Morland took charge in 1932, the 'special' pale blue livery was introduced with car No. 255. This followed the bus livery and the details were as follows:

| | | |
|---|---|---|
| All lower deck panels | : | Pale blue with gold and (inside) white lining with rounded corners. The familiar 'wings' were introduced on either side of the coat of arms. A broad cream band edged in black and lined in pale blue was placed below the windows. |
| All window frames | : | Pale blue. |
| Top deck panels | : | Pale blue with gold and later turquoise lining straight round and a deep cream band below the windows edged in black and lined in pale blue. |
| Trucks and Bumpers etc. | : | Maroon. |
| Roof | : | Grey. |

This livery was used for all the new 'Middleton' cars, Horsfield car 161 and 'Chamberlain' cars 54 and 133, although no other standard cars were so distinguished, and these three were next repainted in the standard blue. In 1935 a modified version was devised for the streamlined four-wheel cars with a deep vee pattern at the ends and they remained in this style for the rest of their service, although the pale blue gave way to royal blue and later red, while No. 272 appeared for a time in plain red, but with the line of the cream bands clearly marked out in black. The lining out was progressively simplified until at the end the cars were unlined. These cars, by design, with London HR2 No. 279 and Middleton Bogie 255 by accident, were the only cars running in Leeds before 1951 which never had cream window frames. The latter two cars remained in the old pale blue livery long enough to be next repainted in the red and cream livery.

In the final period before the war there was a general move toward the simplification of painting styles, especially in reducing the complexity of the lining to cut costs, and Leeds was no exception. Thus by 1939 a single gold line only was used, the 'inside' white lines disappearing, but the corners remained square. The Horsfield cars were given blue rather than cream cantrails.

To meet blackout requirements and conditions all cars not having cream below the lower saloon windows had a broad white band painted round the dash to make them easier to see, bumpers and steps were painted white and headlamps masked. Otherwise painting continued as usual during 1940 and 1941.

A 'war' livery of overall khaki-green with maroon trucks, white bumpers, steps, and a white band on the dash of Hamilton and Chamberlain cars was introduced in 1942. Horsfield cars had the beading below the lower deck cream band painted white whilst Hull cars had that above the rocker panel painted white. This was very drab, and the first cars so painted included No. 339, the last balcony car to be converted, No. 307, the last balcony to be repainted, and all the Hull cars put in service in 1942/3. Of these Nos. 451/71/6 were never painted blue, along with convert 349, while No. 462 was the last grey car to run, not being repainted blue until May 1948. One or two cars were repainted in the full blue and cream during the 1942–44 period. I noted 188 (7/6/43) and 356 (14/11/42). Late grey repaintings were the first retrucked Pivotals (91 and 147, August and July 1944) and ex-Manchester 287 in March 1946.

Blue repainting was resumed in full in February 1944, with cars Nos. 20 (13/2/44) and 90 (27/2/44) and some minor changes were made. The important one was the painting blue of the rocker panels on all cars, the side panel and rocker panel being lined as one entity. Except for converted balcony cars all the corners in the lining became rounded. The pale blue livery was continued for the classes previously so painted, to which was added the Austerity car No. 104 which entered service in 1943 painted pale grey (not the usual khaki-green) with a white band below the upper saloon windows. None of the existing pale blue cars was painted grey.

The new basic livery was thus as follows, although there were some significant variations as described after the main details, which were as follows:

| | |
|---|---|
| Dash Panels<br>Rocker Panels<br>Side panels | : Dark blue, edged in black and lined in deep yellow, with rounded corners. The lining was taken straight past the bulkhead on all the newer smooth sided cars. The Horsfield and all newer cars had a deep cream band below the lower saloon windows, edged in black and lined in dark blue, with the number in small numerals at the side and in large numbers at the end. The side numerals were surrounded by the lining. Converted balcony cars retained the older square corners and a narrow, unlined, band below the lower saloon windows, and at first side numbers. In fact their livery was not altered from their immediate pre-war style. |
| Upper deck panels | : Dark blue, edged in black, and lined in deep yellow, the lining continuing unbroken on all cars except Hamilton enclosed and Chamberlain types. On these the former inconsistencies remained, and an added one was the lining straight round of some Brush and English Electric Chamberlains. All cars except converted balconies had a deep cream band |

| | | |
|---|---|---|
| | | edged in black and lined in dark blue. |
| Window frames and vestibules | : | Cream with medium brown fan light windows and drop window frames on those cars so fitted. The woodwork surrounding the indicator boxes was also brown. |
| Truck, lifeguards etc. | : | Maroon. |
| Roof | : | Grey |

The pale blue cars' livery was modified to have deep yellow lining on the lower deck panels, paler blue on upper deck panels and cream bands with black edging, maroon trucks and grey roofs.

At first the wartime white bands (narrower from 1943), bumpers etc. were retained, but this was discontinued by the autumn of 1944.

From this date activity in the paint shop was sustained at a high level and generally cars were painted inside and out, the adverts being repainted as well, but in later years the inside was often dealt with only every other time, although the inside of the platform was always done.

As adverts were now signwritten direct onto the car ends and sides they had to be painted out when no longer wanted. This resulted in a 'patched' appearance if the lining out was not made good, or expense if the car was 'stopped' a second time for further painting attention. Lining on the top deck blue panels on dark blue cars was omitted, but not in a clean cut way. The first car so treated was Horsfield 197 (4/3/45), the next Horsfield 168 (10/5/46) and the third Hamilton 381 (8/12/46). February, March and April 1947 were months of uncertainty when ten cars were lined and seventeen were plain. Plain panels were then standardised but, as often in Leeds, an exception was made when ex-Manchester 287 was painted blue (24/3/48) and lined, including a break at the bulkheads. Table 1 details the changeover.

It was considered that the cream bands presented a cleaning problem and a better appearance could be maintained without them. A series of experimental liveries were tried during June and July 1948, all lacking cream bands for both dark and pale blue cars and in several cases having lining out only on the dashes. Cream cantrails were also tried and, curiously, the dark blue standard retained full lining and had a blue cantrail whereas the pale blue standard had dash panel lining only and a cream cantrail. The first few had maroon trucks and lifeguards and cream guttering but brown was quickly substituted. These experiments are detailed in Table 2 which also shows that cream paintwork was introduced around the indicators and at first became standard. Unless the route indicator blinds were new, the glass clean and the light good much reduced visibility to intending passengers resulted. Complaints were received and brown painting was reintroduced during February, March and April 1949, again in a rather haphazard way, as detailed in Table 3. Table 4 shows how the change from the large shaded numerals used since 1925 gave way to gill sans ones. It will be noticed that the large numbers were used on older cars latterly.

Another experiment which was unsuccessful was in September 1948 on Horsfield 210 which had dark blue panels and pale blue window frames. I don't think it ran in service in this style and was altered to standard dark blue and cream quickly.

The new standards were:

*Dark Blue Cars*

| | | |
|---|---|---|
| Lower deck panels including dash and rockers | : | Dark blue lined in deep yellow and edged in black |
| Top deck panels | : | Dark blue edged in black |
| Window frames and vestibules | : | Cream. |
| Guttering, trucks and lifeguards | : | Brown. |
| Roof | : | Grey. At first some domed roof cars had silver roofs. Later they were medium blue. |

*Pale Blue Cars*

As above but with silver roof and bow on domed roof cars, brown rather than black edging, lining on the dash only and cream cantrails. Cars with twin headlights had the city coat of arms placed between them and a stylised 'LEEDS CITY TRANSPORT' in the centre of the side panels on Middletons 262/5/6/7/8/71 in gold and 269 in red, also the new 276. This was thereafter replaced by the coat of arms and the usual wings, which were now of the larger type long used on the buses. Additional classes added to the pale blue fleet were the Manchesters, the first car from Southampton (with a grey roof), the new Leeds built double decker and two Horsfields (164, 22/10/48 and 208, 23/1/49). The pale blue was a somewhat different shade from that used previously and in the event did not last at all well.

The last converted balcony car to be repainted (343, 8/48) in the above standard dark blue had some extra cream round the top deck end panels to attempt to lighten its front end appearance.

Early in 1949 several cars (3, 10/2/49; 400, 26/6/49 and 436, 17/4/49 were among them) were painted with a brighter shade of blue, but this was superseded at the start of July by a bright royal blue. Pale blue painting ceased at this time. The only exceptions now to the standard royal blue with cream window frames were 272/3/4 which retained their special style, but in Royal blue.

By the end of the year, however, further change was heralded by the arrival of London Feltham 2099 for trials newly painted in London livery. Soon afterwards it was announced all cars would be repainted red (and the buses green), with the result that from July 1950 several further experimental liveries were tried. Some cars were all over red, one scarlet with narrow buff bands, three had a red version of the standard blue, and there was wide variety in the amount of lining out. Table 5 gives the details. The standard was achieved in October 1950 thus:

| | | |
|---|---|---|
| Lower deck panels and all window frames | : | Crimson, lower deck and dash panels lined in deep yellow. All cars had a cream band below the windows, which was deeper and lined in red on classes C, D, E, F and UCC (dash only). |
| Upper deck panels | : | Crimson. All cars except H, and UCC had a deep |

| | |
|---|---|
| | cream band lined in red below the window frames. H, and UCC had a narrow unlined cream band. |
| Fan lights, indicator woodwork, trucks, lifeguards | : Brown. |
| Guttering | : Black. |
| Roof | : Grey. |

The following exceptions need to be noted. Austerity 275 had both cream bands lined whilst 276 had both plain. Southampton 290 had both bands lined and ex London 301 the lower deck one only.

Feltham cars had an area of cream above the lower saloon windows. 425 was the first Leeds built Chamberlain to be painted red in October 1951and, because of the way the vestibule was built, could not have the cream band round the dash. It was therefore applied on the side panel only and this was adopted as a new standard for Chamberlain cars until Manchester 281 came in for painting in April 1952 when it could not be applied at all on the very narrow waist panel on these cars. It was omitted altogether and this was also standardised immediately.

Further simplification took place by substitution of red for the brown indicator woodwork and fan lights, detailed in Table 6, and a reduction in width of the upper deck cream band on the Middletons, then lacking lining.

During February 1951 freshly overhauled Feltham car No. 525 and HR2 No. 278, after equipping with air brakes and major overhaul, were painted in vermilion rather than crimson followed in April by Feltham 531 and May by 538. Thereafter this was not repeated, nor was the use of a royal blue version of the standard red painting style on Chamberlain-Pivotal cars 35, 69 and 133 about the same time.

The additional painting cost of the lining out must have been considerable, and greater than in the final blue days, so that some economy was almost inevitable. This began at the end of May 1952 with the final wave of experimental paintings. In these lining out was omitted, some cars had pale green bands, some had light jade green bands and some were plain red, but still with the black edging where the cream bands would have been. In the experiments two cars were painted in the standard colours without any lining, which was adopted as the new standard, and all those with green and jade bands had them overpainted cream, as had most of the plain red ones. Five plain red ones remained, three not being repainted before withdrawal, the other two being fully repainted in 1953 and 1954. Full details form Table 7.

During the remaining five years in which cars were repainted there was a further reduction in the amount of black edging applied, whilst different roof colours were introduced with the 1952 experiments, a red-brown colour for flat roofed cars and a lighter greenish-grey for domed roof cars.

The Roe built single deckers 601/2 however, just spoilt the picture, for, entering service in Coronation month, June 1953, they were specially painted in royal purple, with black edging, real gold lining on the purple panels, ivory window frames and bow collector tower, and brown bogies. The roofs were purple. They were never subsequently repainted. The final single deck car, No.

600 placed in service in August 1954, was in crimson with cream window frames, unlined, and with a pale grey roof.

The further economy in black was introduced from April 1954 when the black edging was reduced to that necessary to separate the cream from the red, the guttering becoming red also, and Chamberlain cars (60, 74/6, 84, 93, 124/39) painted in July 1955 were without the black between the rocker panel and the truck, which actually looked better. Towards the end of operations more and more patch repainting was resorted to, and the last cars to be fully redone were two of the original experimental Leeds Horsfields, Nos. 153/4 which were dealt with in July 1958, in a rather brighter shade of red. Both these cars were withdrawn on 29 March 1959, although No. 153 was working on the Briggate–Moortown service on the last evening.

LIVERIES – TABLE 1
Introduction of unlined upper deck blue panels Feb–April 1947

| Date | Car | U/L = unlined S = standard | Date | Car | U/L or S | Date | Car | U/L or S |
|---|---|---|---|---|---|---|---|---|
| 1.2.47 | 24 | S | 6.3.47 | 210 | U/L | 30.3.47 | 211 | U/L |
| 1.2.47 | 95 | U/L | 6.3.47 | 411 | U/L | 30.3.47 | 227 | S |
| 4.2.47 | 203 | S | 9.3.47 | 192 | S | 6.4.47 | 159 | U/L |
| 9.2.47 | 220 | S | 9.3.47 | 222 | S | 6.4.47 | 199 | U/L |
| 9.2.47 | 248 | S | 13.3.47 | 231 | U/L | 6.4.47 | 419 | U/L |
| 23.2.47 | 129 | S | 14.3.47 | 167 | U/L | 6.4.47 | 427 | S |
| 1.3.47 | 170 | U/L | 23.3.47 | 180 | U/L | 20.4.47 | 242 | U/L |
| 1.3.47 | 179 | U/L | 23.3.47 | 430 | U/L | 27.4.47 | 218 | U/L |
| 4.3.47 | 448 | S | 23.3.47 | 450 | U/L | 27.4.47 | 428 | U/L |

LIVERIES – TABLE 2
Experimental liveries June–July 1948

| Date | Car | Livery variation |
|---|---|---|
| 13.6.48 | 144 | No cream band, lined on dash only |
| 13.6.48 | 197 | No cream bands, lined on dash only |
| 20.6.48 | 403 | No cream band, cream indicator woodwork |
| 22.6.48 | 66 | No cream band |
| 26.6.48 | 277 | Pale blue panels, cream window frames and route number indicator woodwork. No cream bands, black edging, lined on dash only, cream cantrail, Gill Sans numbers, brown bogies and lifeguards |
| Not given | 199 | No cream bands, lined on dash only, cream cantrail |
| Not given | 173 | No cream bands, cream cantrail |
| 30.6.48 | 31 | No cream band, lined on dash only |
| 4.7.48 | 23 | No cream band, cream end indicator woodwork |
| 4.7.48 | 49 | No cream band, cream end indicator woodwork |

LIVERIES – TABLE 2—continued

| Date | Car | Livery variation |
|---|---|---|
| 5.7.48 | 160 | No cream bands, cream end indicator woodwork, Gill Sans numbers, no side numbers |
| 5.7.48 | 254 | No cream bands |
| 11.7.48 | 92 | No cream band, cream end indicator woodwork |
| 18.7.48 | 79 | No cream band, cream end indicator woodwork |
| 18.7.48 | 412 | No cream band, cream end indicator woodwork |
| 18.7.48 | 189 | No cream bands, cream end indicator woodwork, Gill Sans numbers, no side numbers |
| 23.7.48 | 150 | No cream band |
| 25.7.48 | 5 | No cream band, cream end indicator woodwork |
| 25.7.48 | 258 | Pale blue panels, cream window frames, no cream bands, lined on dash only, large numbers between headlights, brown lifeguards and bogies. |

LIVERIES – TABLE 3

Re-introduction of brown end indicator woodwork March 1949

| Date | Car | Ind. woodwork colour | Date | Car | Ind. woodwork colour |
|---|---|---|---|---|---|
| 4.3.49 | 138 | Cream | 19.3.49 | 200 | Brown |
| 4.3.49 | 387 | Cream | 19.3.49 | 213 | Cream |
| 9.3.49 | 243 | Cream | 19.3.49 | 97 | Cream |
| 14.3.49 | 203 | Cream | 20.3.49 | 74 | Cream |
| 19.3.49 | 244 | Brown | 20.3.49 | 74 | Cream |

and all cars in April – Brown: 8, 15, 48, 142/9, 218/24, 399, 436

LIVERIES – TABLE 4

Changeover from large to Gill Sans numerals

| | | |
|---|---|---|
| August 1948 | Large numbers | – 60, 89, 94, 105/12, 408/34 |
| | Gill Sans | – 152, 252 |
| September 1948 | Large numbers | – 102, 390 |
| | Gill Sans | – 210/76/81 |
| October 1948 | Large numbers | – 33, 59, 371/92, 445 |
| | Gill Sans | – 164/8/95, 271/82 |
| 1 November 1948 | Large numbers | – 35, 58, 393 |
| November 1948 | Gill Sans | – 21, 106/63, 246/83, 409 |

and all cars thereafter Gill Sans

LIVERIES – TABLE 5

Experimental liveries July to November 1950 introducing red paint. 2099 ran in London livery from December 1949 until due for repainting

| Date | Car | Livery |
|---|---|---|
| .7.50 | 256 | Deep crimson all over including roof and bow collector. No lining but black edging fully applied as on the former pale blue cream banded livery. Black guttering, bogies, life-guards etc. Front coat of arms retained |
| .7.50 | 269 | Scarlet, no lining or edging, black bogies, steps, life-guards etc. Front coat of arms retained. A narrow buff band below upper and lower deck windows. Silver roof and bow |
| .9.50 | 502 | Deep crimson panelling, medium green window frames (excluding any areas above or below the framework), black edging bogies and lifeguards, dark grey roof. This car was altered to the style detailed below for 4/10/50 before running in regular service |
| 17.9.50 | 99 | Crimson panels and cream window frames lined and edged as the standard royal blue but with black trucks and lifeguards. The inside of the platform vestibules was red rather than cream. Black solebar |
| 24.9.50 | 153 | Crimson panelling and frames, deep yellow lining round the lower deck panels and double yellow lining round the former top deck cream band. Black guttering, truck and lifeguards. Brown indicator woodwork, fanlights and grey roof |
| 1.10.50 | 85 | As 99 but with additional top deck lining as 153 |
| 1.10.50 | 226 | As 99 |
| 2.10.50 | 141 | As 153, but only a single yellow line at the top of the former top deck cream band. Black solebar |
| 4.10.50 | 502 | Crimson panelling and window frames, deep yellow lining round the dash and lower deck side panels. A narrow cream band below the upper saloon windows and a broad cream area above the lower saloon windows. Fully edged in black, black bogies, lifeguards etc. Black roof |
| .10.50 | 266 | As 153 |
| 4.10.50 | 503 | As 153 with one deep yellow line below the upper saloon windows |
| 10.10.50 | 264 | As 503 |
| 17.10.50 | 238 | As 503 |
| 24.10.50 | 505 | As 502 (4.10.50 version) |
| 25.10.50 | 504 | As 502 (4.10.50 version) |
| 25.10.50 | 16 | As 141 |
| 25.10.50 | 157 | Crimson panels and window frames with full black edging lined on the lower deck in deep yellow. Deep |

| Date | Car | Livery |
|---|---|---|
| | | cream bands below upper and lower saloon windows lined in crimson. Black guttering but brown trucks, indicator woodwork, lifeguards and fanlights. Grey roof and bow collector, gold number on cream band. New fixed top deck window frames and Pullman ventilators, polished medium oak |
| 21.10.50 | 299 | Crimson panels and window frames with full black edging lined on the lower deck panels in deep yellow. Narrow unlined cream band below upper saloon windows. Black edging, truck and lifeguards, brown indicator surround and fanlights. Grey roof |
| 25.10.50 | 67 | As 299 but with a normal width cream band below the upper saloon windows lined in crimson. Black solebar |
| 29.10.50 | 169 | As 157 |
| 7.11.50 | 506 | As 502 but with a broad cream band round the drivers cab, with the number on it in gold and lined in crimson. Brown bogies, lifeguards etc. Grey roof |
| 12.11.50 | 235 | As 157 |
| 12.11.50 | 167 | As 157 |
| 12.11.50 | 229 | As 157 |
| 14.11.50 | 507 | As 502 (4.10.50 version) |
| 19.11.50 | 35 | As 67 but with royal blue instead of crimson |
| 19.11.50 | 298 | Former standard royal blue and cream |
| 26.11.50 | 72 | As 67 but with a narrow cream band below the lower saloon windows, lined in crimson. The truck and lifeguards were brown, but the solebars black |
| 26.11.50 | 71 | As 72 but with the lower cream band unlined |
| .12.50 | 509 | As 506 but with cream window frames and no upper deck cream bands |

Nos 71, 157 and 506 were adopted as the new standard

LIVERIES – TABLE 6
Introduction of red indicator woodwork and fanlights

| Date | Car | Colour | Date | Car | Colour | Date | Car | Colour |
|---|---|---|---|---|---|---|---|---|
| 6.5.51 | 4 | Brown | 24.6.51 | 181 | Brown | 1.7.51 | 173 | Brown |
| 20.5.51 | 83 | Red | .6.51 | 244 | Red | 1.7.51 | 194 | Red |
| 3.6.51 | 81 | Brown | 22.7.51 | 39 | Brown | 1.7.51 | 247 | Brown |
| 10.6.51 | 65 | Red | 29.7.51 | 49 | Red | 15.7.51 | 201 | Red |
| 19.6.51 | 204 | Red | | | | | | |

Horsfield cars newly fitted with Pullman ventilators etc retained the light oak polished frames

LIVERIES – TABLE 7
Experimental liveries June–July 1952 to determine 'unlined' standards

| Date | Car | Livery |
|---|---|---|
| 25.5.52 | 219 | Crimson panels and window frames, black edging, trucks, lifeguards and guttering. Cream bands replaced by very light green. No lining |
| 1.6.52 | 242 | As 219 but with brown truck and lifeguard |
| 8.6.52 | 196 | As 242 |
| 8.6.52 | 1 | As 242 but with only the top deck band, normal for Chamberlains |
| 8.6.52 | 36 | As 1 |
| 8.6.52 | 29 | As 1 but with a pale jade green or turquoise band |
| 22.6.52 | 70 | Crimson all over fully edged as the 'banded' cars. No lining, reddish brown roof and bow |
| 22.6.52 | 28 | Crimson panels and window frames, and cream band. As former standard but unlined |
| 25.6.52 | 270 | As 70 but with a grey roof |
| 25.6.52 | 272 | As 70 but with a grey roof |
| 29.6.52 | 146 | as 70 |
| 29.6.52 | 166 | As 29 but with two turquoise bands |
| 6.7.52 | 186 | As 70 |
| 6.7.52 | 253 | As 70 |
| 6.7.52 | 130 | As 29 |
| 13.7.52 | 132 | As 70 |
| 13.7.52 | 220 | As 28 but with two cream bands, normal for Horsfields |
| 10.8.52 | 283 | As 70 but with a greenish grey roof |

Nos 28 and 220 were selected for the new standard with the red/brown roof colour. Domed roof cars had the same roof colour as 283. Only Horsfield and EXHR2 cars now had a wide upper deck cream band. Of the above experiments the green or jade bands were overpainted cream by the end of August, 132 and 253 had cream bands added by the end of August. The others remained as they were – 70, 146 and 283 until withdrawn and 186, 270 and 272 until repainted by September 1954.

APPENDIX B1

# Horse and steam trailer cars operated by Leeds Tramways Company 1871–94 and Leeds Corporation 1894–1902

Until the publication in 1985 of Vol 1 of 'Leeds Transport' by J. Soper incorporating most painstaking research by the Leeds Transport Historical Society, the only published details of the horse and steam trailer cars used in Leeds were in the City Engineers 1895 report. The research showed the totals for each type of car to be incorrect, but they also disagree with the totals given by the Tramways Company's legal representative at the Arbitration in 1893, themselves different from those in the City Engineers report. The following details are therefore summarised from 'Leeds Transport Vol 1'.

*Horse Trailers*
Single deck cars, one horse, weighed 1 ton 8 cwt or 1 ton 11 cwt, double deck cars, two or three horses, weighed 2 tons 4 cwt or 2 tons 6 cwt and had outside stairs and open platforms. All the cars had 30″ diameter chilled iron disc wheels.

*1871 Nos 1–4*

| | | | |
|---|---|---|---|
| Builder | : Starbuck | Type | : Double deck |
| Wheelbase | : 6′0″ | Seats | : 20.20:40 |
| No. of cars | : 5 | | |

Nos 2, 3 to LCT 1894, became Nos 49, 52 in 1897
Others withdrawn 1885/6

*1871–2 Nos 5–14*

| | | | |
|---|---|---|---|
| Builder | : Stephenson | Type | : Double deck |
| Wheelbase | : 6′0″ | Seats | : 24.24:48 No. 7 |
| | 5′6″ Nos 9, 10, 13 | | 24.22:46 No. 5, later 6 |
| | | | 22.22:44 Nos 5, 11, 12, 14 |
| | | | 22.20:42 No. 8 |
| No. of cars | : 10 | | 20.18:38 Nos 9, 10 |
| | | | 18.18:36 No. 13 |

No. 5 (the first) renumbered 6 November 1871
Nos 6, 8 to LCT 1894, became 55, 76 in 1897
Others withdrawn: 4 in 1873, 4 in 1876

*1873 Nos 15–18*

| | | | |
|---|---|---|---|
| Builder | : Starbuck | Type | : Double deck |
| Wheelbase | : 6′0″ | Seats | : 20.20:40 |
| No. of cars | : 4 | | |

Nos 17, 18 to LCT 1894, became 85, 86 in 1897
Others sold 1873

*1873 Nos 19, 20*

| | | | |
|---|---|---|---|
| Builder | : Starbuck | Type | : Single deck |
| Wheelbase | : 5′6″ | Seats | : 16 No. 20<br>14 No. 19 |
| No. of cars | : 2 | | |

Withdrawn 1876

*1873 Nos 21–26*

| | | | |
|---|---|---|---|
| Builder | : Starbuck | Type | : Double deck |
| Wheelbase | : 6′0″ | Seats | : 20.20:40 |
| No. of cars | : 5 | | |

Nos 24–26 renumbered 5, 7, 9 in 1874, not necessarily respectively
Nos 22, 23 to LCT 1894, became Nos 90, 91 in 1897
Others withdrawn 1886/7

*1874 Nos 10, 24–31*

| | | | |
|---|---|---|---|
| Builder | : Starbuck | Type | : Double deck |
| Wheelbase | : 5′6″ | Seats | : 16.16:32 |
| No. of cars | : 9 | | |

No. 26 withdrawn 1888
Others to LCT 1894, Nos 10, 24, 25 became 78, 92, 93 in 1897

*1874–6 Nos 11–16, ? 19, ? 20, 32–51*

| | | | |
|---|---|---|---|
| Builder | : Starbuck | Type | : Single deck |
| Wheelbase | : 5′6″ | Seats | : 18 |
| No. of cars | : 28 | | |

Nos ?19, ?20 withdrawn 1885/6
Nos 13, 33/5–8/41/7/9 withdrawn 1888–9
Nos 11, 12, 14–16 to LCT 1894 became 79, 80, 82–84 in 1897
Nos 32/4/9, 40/2–6/8/50/1 to LCT 1894

*1879 Nos 52–54*

| | | | |
|---|---|---|---|
| Builder | : LTC at Headingley | Type | : Open |
| Wheelbase | : 5′6″ | Seats | : 24, later 22 |
| No. of cars | : 3 | | |

Withdrawn 1881 (1) 1885/6 (2)

*1883 Nos 56–58*

| | | | |
|---|---|---|---|
| Builder | : Ashbury | Type | : Double deck, Eades 'Reversible' |
| Wheelbase | : 5′6″ | | |
| No. of cars | : 3 | Seats | : 20.18:38 |

These cars had only one platform and staircase, the body revolving on the frame when reversal was required.
All to LCT 1894

*1887 Nos 67–68*

| | | | |
|---|---|---|---|
| Builder | : LTC at North Street | Type | : Double deck |
| Wheelbase | : 6′0″ | Seats | : 20.20:40 |
| No. of cars | : 2 | | |

Fitted with 'garden' seats top deck
Both to LCT 1894

*1887 Nos 69–70*

| | | | |
|---|---|---|---|
| Builder | : Milnes | Type | : Double deck |
| Wheelbase | : 6′0″ | Seats | : Not known |
| No. of cars | : 2 | | |

Fitted with garden seats, top deck.
Both to LCT 1894

*1887 No. 74*

| | | | |
|---|---|---|---|
| Builder | : Milnes | Type | : Single deck |
| Wheelbase | : 5′6″ | Seats | : 18 |
| No. of cars | : 1 | | |

To LCT 1894

*1887 Nos 1, 7, 9*

| | | | |
|---|---|---|---|
| Builder | : Milnes | Type | : Single deck |
| Wheelbase | : 5′6″ | Seats | : 16 |
| No. of cars | : 3 | | |

All to LCT 1894, 1 becoming 47, 7, 75 and 9, 77 in 1897
Several cars were rebuilt by the Leeds Tramways Company 1880–89.

*Steam Trailers*
Double deck top covered bogie cars with open platforms and outside stairs. Nos 55, 59 and 60 were delivered as four wheelers but were quickly placed on bogies. All the bogies were of the plate frame type and, except for Nos 61/2 which had 21″ diameter wheels, had 24″ wheels. All passed to LCT in 1894, but 55 was in very poor condition and probably never used. It was withdrawn and scrapped in 1895.

*1882 No. 55*

| | | | |
|---|---|---|---|
| Builder | : Ashbury | Seats | : Not known |
| No. of cars | : 1 | | |

Eades 'Reversible' design. Partly top covered.

*1883–4 Nos 59–62*

| | | | |
|---|---|---|---|
| Builder | : Starbuck | Seats | : 24.22:46 |
| No. of cars | : 4 | | |

No. 60 converted to single deck by LCT 1895

*1885–6 Nos 63–66*

| | | | |
|---|---|---|---|
| Builder | : Starbuck | Seats | : 28.26:54 |
| No. of cars | : 4 | | |

Nos 63, 66 converted to single deck by LCT 1895

*1887 Nos 71–3*

| | | | |
|---|---|---|---|
| Builder | : Ashbury | Seats | : 34.26:60 |
| No. of cars | : 3 | | |

*1888 Nos 4, 5, 13, 20, 21, 26, 33, 35–8, 41*

| | | | |
|---|---|---|---|
| Builder | : Milnes | Seats | : 38.28:66 |
| No. of cars | : 12 | | |

Nos 4, 5, 13, 20 and 21 became 53, 54, 88 and 89 in 1897

*Horse Trailers purchased by Leeds Corporation*

*1897–8 Nos 50, 78, 93–7, 105–10*

| | | | |
|---|---|---|---|
| Builder | : Milnes | Type | : Double deck |
| Wheelbase | : 5′6″ | Seats | : 18.16:34 |
| No. of cars | : 13 | | |

*1898–9 Nos 111–20*

| | | | |
|---|---|---|---|
| Builder | : Milnes | Type | : Single deck |
| Wheelbase | : 5′6″ | Seats | : 18 |
| No. of cars | : 10 | | |

Apart from one or two in particularly poor condition withdrawn in 1897 all the trailer cars were taken out of service 1899 to 1902.

## APPENDIX B2

# Works cars operated by Leeds Corporation

The first recorded works cars used by Leeds Corporation were the original Roundhay line cars which were adapted for that purpose in 1900, being described as salt cars. These were supplanted in the twenties by cars modified from the early withdrawals, which were mainly of the 1899 Brush series, reduced to single deck. One Dick Kerr car (vestibuled) survived as No. 8A until the end of operation, although I never saw it on the road.

This second generation of cars was replaced in the late thirties by two new ones adapted in 1936 from 1904 Brush cars. These were altered by removal of the top deck and stairs, boarding up the sides and fitting a large sliding door in the middle. The cars were vestibuled (they had been as passenger cars) and were distinguished by having twin headlamps. The bow collectors were mounted on a tower. They were given numbers 2 and 3 in the Stores car Series and after the war at least had on the sides 'P.W.Dept, Stores Car'. The older cars were not immediately withdrawn, but, except 8A as mentioned above, did not survive the war.

Certain of the tippler cars were transferred in the twenties to permanent way duties and the last of these was No. 4 which remained, minus its hoppers, at Torre Road depot yard in 1948, equipped with a bow collector. No doubt these cars retained numbers in the separate series they had when in commercial service.

The extension of reserved tracks created problems with overhead maintenance, which had been undertaken by a motor tower wagon from about 1910, and presumably by a horse wagon before that, so that about 1930 a tower car was built on the frame of an old car. It had a square wooden body with a tower and later two bow collectors, being mounted on a Peckham cantilever truck. It bore the number 1. To supplement this car Chamberlain No. 420 was modified after its withdrawal in May 1953 to become overhead wire car 2. The top deck window frames and the roof were removed and two towers, each with a bow collector, were constructed.

Rail grinding was another activity having special cars, a rotary grinder being constructed in 1906 on the frame of a steam tram engine, its origins being discernible, with metal skirting down to road level. This continued at work for the remaining period of tramway operation. A second car was modified in 1939 from one of the last 1900 English Electric cars, which was reduced to single deck, fitted with twin headlights, and vestibuled (this may have existed before) similarly to Stores cars 2 and 3. This second car had reciprocating equipment by the Equipment and Engineering Company, a circumstance resulting from Mr. Vane Morland's visit to America.

Snow clearance was a necessity at some time during most winters, and although normal road clearance assisted increasingly as the years went by, heavy falls needed attention on the reserved track sections. Three snowbrooms, numbered 1–3 were maintained for this purpose, being purpose built machines, single deck with the body frame mounted very much above normal height above the track. The bodies bore some design similarity to the 1906 rail grinder.

One of the first 1908/9 Hamilton cars to be withdrawn was modified about 1937 as a water car, being given the number 5. Apart from removal of the top deck and stairs it received little external alteration, and unlike other works cars modified at this period retained single headlights.

An interesting addition to the stores car fleet was Hull No. 96 which was transferred to Leeds with the final batch of Hull passenger cars in 1945, becoming Leeds Works car 6. This was a single decker of very typical Hull outline with a three window body of Tudor arch design and a Brill truck. It ran to the end of operations in Leeds. It was retained and is now restored as a single deck passenger car running on the Heaton Park Tramway in Manchester.

The cars so far described were painted in a medium grey with white numbers, but in the early fifties Stores car 3 and Rail Grinder 1 were painted in buff with a red stripe edged in brown and brown lettering and trucks.

Between 1951 and 1955 certain passenger cars were transferred to service use without modification, repainting or renumbering as follows:

Chamberlain 83, withdrawn 20 November 1955, as a snow blade, with fixed snow blades in place of lifeguards

Hamilton 399, withdrawn 27 September 1951 as Kirkstall Road Works shunter.

Hamilton 377 withdrawn 11 June 1952 for transferring items between Swinegate and Kirkstall Road Works.

## APPENDIX B3

# Electric passenger cars operated in Leeds 1891–1959

The following notes provide full details of the Electric cars, including the 1948 classification where appropriate. The following abbreviations are used for manufacturers of equipment etc.

BTH – British Thomson Houston Limited
DK – Dick Kerr Limited
EMB – Electro Mechanical Brake Company Limited
GEC – General Electric Company Limited
LCT – Leeds City Tramways – later Transport
M&T – Maley and Taunton Limited
MV – Metropolitan Vickers Limited
SKF – Skefco Ball Bearing Company Limited

Seating capacities are given in each case – upper deck . lower deck: total

*1891 Hackney Carriages Committee Licence Nos 75–80*

Built to the designs of John Stephenson, in New York, open platformed canopied single deckers. Operated by the Thomson-Houston Company under a concession over Corporation constructed tracks.

| | | | |
|---|---|---|---|
| No. of cars | 6 | Wheel diameter | 30″ |
| Motors | SRG 30B | Bearings | Plain |
| Gear ratio | 67:14 | Brakes | Hand, electric emergency |
| Truck | Bemis Std 26 | Controllers | – |
| Wheelbase | 6′0″ | Seats | 22 |

Withdrawn from passenger service 31 July 1896 when Sheepscar–Oakwood and Harehills Road sections closed for re-equipment.

Purchased by Leeds Corporation for use as trailers with electric cars 1898, numbered 121–7. Such use discontinued in 1900 when these cars were converted to works use as salt cars.

Trailers 121–7 included an open sided trailer built for the Roundhay line in 1895 of which little detail and no number information is available.

*1897 Nos 1–25*
Milnes bodied, uncanopied, open top double deckers, erected by Greenwood and Batley, Leeds.

| | | | |
|---|---|---|---|
| No. of cars | 25 | Wheel Diameter | 32″ |
| Motors | BTH GE 800 | Bearings | Plain |
| Gear ratio | – | Brakes | Hand and electric emergency |
| Truck | Peckham Cantilever | Controllers | BTH K2 |
| Wheelbase | 6′0″ | Seats | 28.22:50 |

Four window bodies with 'Tudor Arch' windows.

Rebuilt from 1906 with full canopies, new standard stairs and fan light style canopied top covers. Seating capacity altered to 34.22:56.

Most vestibuled from 1910 and some latterly equipped with DK DB series controllers and Brill 21E trucks.

Those running after 1926 renumbered with 'A' suffix.

Withdrawn between 1928 and 1936.

*1899 Nos. 85, 90, 133–82*
Brush uncanopied, open top, double deckers.

| | | | |
|---|---|---|---|
| No. of cars | 52 | Wheel diameter | 32″ |
| Motors | BTH GE 58 | Bearings | Plain |
| Gear ratio | 68:16 | Brakes | Hand, electric emergency, †magnetic track |
| Truck | Peckham Cantilever | | |
| Wheelbase | 6′0″ | Controllers | BTH K2, †BTH B13 |
| | | Seats | 32.22:54 |

Four window bodies with 'Tudor Arch' windows.

Rebuilt with short top covers 1906–13.

Nos. 85, 90 with 'round arch' windows, magnetic track brakes and BTH B13 controllers.

Nos. 150–9 with magnetic track brakes and BTH B13 controllers.

No. 133/8/47/8/63/70/7/80 hired by West Riding Tramways 1917, bought 1919, out of stock LCT 1920.

Those of Nos. 134–50 running after 1926 renumbered with 'A' suffix.

Withdrawn 1925–28.

*1900 Nos. 98–103, 128–32*
Originally built as trailers 1897, uncanopied, open top double deckers. Rebuilt as electric cars 1900.

| | | | |
|---|---|---|---|
| No. of cars | 11 | Wheel diameter | 32″ |
| Motors | BTH GE 58 | Bearings | Plain |

| | | | |
|---|---|---|---|
| Gear ratio | 68:16 | Brakes | Hand, electric emergency |
| Truck | Peckham Cantilever | Controllers | BTH K10 |
| Wheelbase | 6′0″ | Seats | 28.20:48 |

Nos. 98–103 built by Milnes with four window 'Tudor Arch' bodies.

Nos. 128–32 built by Brush with four window 'Tudor Arch' bodies.

Rebuilt 1906–13 with short top covers.

Those running after 1926 renumbered with 'A' suffix.

Withdrawn 1925–28.

*1900 Nos. 44, 46, 55, 79, 83*
Brush uncanopied, open top cars built for Liverpool (Nos. 464–8) but returned by them and bought by Leeds.

| | | | |
|---|---|---|---|
| No. of cars | 5 | Wheel diameter | 32″ |
| Motors | BTH GE 800A | Bearings | Plain |
| Gear ratio | – | Brakes | Hand, Westinghouse magnetic |
| Truck | Brush | Controllers | BTH K10 |
| Wheelbase | 6′0″ | Seats | 32.22:54 |

Four window bodies, rebuilt 1906–13 with short top covers.

Those running after 1926 renumbered with 'A' suffix.

Withdrawn 1925–28.

*1900 No. 49*
Brill convertible single decker, purchased after display at Tramway and Light Railway Exhibition. Canopied and with side panels which could be raised to the roof.

| | | | |
|---|---|---|---|
| No. of cars | 1 | Wheel diameter | 32″ |
| Motors | BTH GE 58 | Bearings | Plain |
| Gear ratio | 68:16 | Brakes | Hand, emergency electric |
| Truck | Brill 21E | Controllers | BTH K10 |
| Wheelbase | 6′0″ | Seats | 29 |

Withdrawn 1914.

*1900 No. 52*
Brush uncanopied, open top round arch five window double deck bogie car purchased after experiments with the Anderson surface contact system in Beckett Street.

| | | | |
|---|---|---|---|
| No. of cars | 1 | Wheel diameter | 32″ and ? |
| Motors | BTH GE 58 | Bearings | Plain |
| Gear ratio | 68:16 | Brakes | Hand, emergency electric |
| Bogies | Brill maximum traction | Controllers | BTH K10 |
| Wheelbase | – | Seats | 36.26:62 |

Mounted on Brill 21E 6′0″ four wheel truck before 1906 with DK EE 35A motors. Later equipped with a long wheelbase truck.

Rebuilt between 1906 and 13 with a totally enclosed short top cover.

Renumbered with 'A' suffix 1926.

Withdrawn 1928.

*1901 Nos. 183–282*
Dick Kerr canopied open top double deckers with three window fan light ventilator bodies and reversed stairs.

| | | | |
|---|---|---|---|
| No. of cars | 100 | Wheel diameter | 32″ |
| Motors | DK EE.35A | Bearings | Plain |
| Gear ratio | – | Brakes | Hand, emergency electric †magnetic track |
| Truck | Brill 21E | Controllers | DK.DE1 †BTH K10 |
| Wheelbase | 6′0″ | Seats | 36.22:58 |

12 cars equipped with BTH K10 controllers and magnetic track brakes.

50 cars rebuilt with canopied four window, drop window top covers 1903–06.

49 cars rebuilt with canopied four window fan light ventilated top covers 1906–13.

No.231 fitted with canopied four window fan light ventilated top cover 1921.

No. 270 first car fitted with Maley mechanical track brakes in 1907, a number of others thereafter fitted.

No. 184 experimentally modified as front entrance car in 1914 and vestibuled. Withdrawn in 1915 but not taken out of stock until 1920.

Some vestibuled or partially vestibuled, the latter after 1919.

Many cars later fitted with DK DB1 K3 controllers and some mounted on Peckham cantilever trucks.

Cars running after 1931 renumbered with 'A' suffix except Nos. 275–82.

Withdrawn 1928–38, one of the last ones being converted to a works car.

*1902 Nos. 27–32/4/9, 40/2/3/5/7/8, 50/1/6–8, 67–9, 70/4–8, 80/2/4/6/7, 91–7, 104–13*
Brush canopied open top double deckers with three window fan light ventilator bodies and reversed stairs.

| | | | |
|---|---|---|---|
| No. of cars | 50 | Wheel diameter | 32″ |
| Motors | BTH GE 58 | Bearings | Plain |
| Gear ratio | 68:16 | Brakes | Hand, emergency electric or Westinghouse magnetic track |
| Truck | Peckham Cantilever | Controllers | BTH K10 BTH B18 |
| Wheelbase | 6′0″ | Seats | 36.20:56 |

All fitted with canopied four window drop window top covers 1903–6, after experiments with other types on cars 51 and 82 in 1902.

38 cars with Westinghouse magnetic track brakes and BTH B18 controllers.

Most vestibuled 1910–15.

Nos. 87, 104–11 modified for dual gauge working to Bradford 1909–18.

Some later equipped with DK DB1 K3 controllers.

Those running after 1926 renumbered with 'A' suffix.

Withdrawn 1928–38.

*1904 Nos. 26, 33/5, 41, 53/4/9, 60–6, 71–3, 81/8/9, 114/27*
Brush canopied double deckers with three window fan light ventilator bodies, canopied four window, drop window top covers and standard stairs.

| | | | |
|---|---|---|---|
| No. of cars | 25 | Wheel diameter | 32″ |
| Motors | BTH GE 58 | Bearings | Plain |
| Gear ratio | 68:16 | Brakes | Hand, Westinghouse magnetic track |
| Truck | Brush | Controllers | BTH B18 |
| Wheelbase | 6′0″ | Seats | 34.22:56 |

Vestibuled 1910–15.

Some later equipped with DK DB1 K3 controllers.

41, 73 and some others reconstructed 1928–30, receiving fan light top covers.

Those running after 1926 renumbered with 'A' suffix.

Withdrawn 1928–38, some of the last being converted to works cars.

*1908–09 Nos. 115–26*
Hamilton designed, Leeds built double deckers with open balconies and unvestibuled.

| | | | |
|---|---|---|---|
| No. of cars | 12 | Wheel diameter | 32″ |
| Motors | DK 9A | Bearings | Plain |
| Gear ratio | 68:16 | Brakes | Hand, rheostatic |
| Truck | Brill 21E | Controllers | DK DB1 K1 |
| Wheelbase | 6′6″ | Seats | 38.24:62 |

Nos. 115/6 built 1908 with reversed stairs, remainder in 1909 with standard stairs.

All later equipped with DK DB1 K3 controllers.

All vestibuled 1910–15.

Renumbered 1926/7 with 'A' suffix.

No. 116A rebuilt February 1938 with M&T air track brakes, Mechanical Track Brakes, MV 114 motors, 67:14 gears, Peckham P.22 truck, totally enclosed (seats 42.24:66) with new stairs, platform doors and flush panelled sides. Classed A3/MV 114 in 1948. Renumbered 275 in 1938, 349 in 1948 and withdrawn February 1951.

No. 119A rebuilt similar to 116A May 1939 but with BTH 510H controllers, Hurst Nelson 7′6″ wheelbase truck and 30 B1 motors. Classed A2/510H in 1948. Renumbered 276 in 1939 and 342 in 1948, and withdrawn July 1949.

No. 125A sold to Rotherham 1939.

One became Water Car 5 in 1939.

Remainder withdrawn: 3 in 1938/9, 6 in 1945.

*1911–12 Nos. 283–292*
Hamilton designed, Leeds built double deckers, vestibuled but with open top deck balconies. Detail differences from Nos. 115–26, including reversed stairs.

| | | | |
|---|---|---|---|
| No. of cars | 10 | Wheel diameter | 32″ |
| Motors | BTH GE 58, DK9A | Bearings | Plain |
| Gear ratio | 68:16 | Brakes | Hand, rheostatic, Maley mechanical track |
| Truck | Brill 21E | Controllers | DK DB1 K3 |
| Wheelbase | 6′6″, 7′6″ | Seats | 36.22:58 |

Nos. 283–5 with DK 9A motors in 1945.

Nos. 289–91 with 6′6″ wheelbase in 1945.

Nos. 285–8 with Maley mechanical track brakes in 1945.

Withdrawn 1945, except 291 dismantled for firewatching purposes about 1940.

No. 288 sold for use as a bungalow.

*1913–15 Nos. 293–339*
Hamilton designed, Leeds built double deckers vestibuled but with open top deck balconies. Flatter front ends, deeper top deck side panels modified vestibules compared with 283–292. Reversed stairs.

| | | | |
|---|---|---|---|
| No. of cars | 47 | Wheel diameter | 32″ |
| Motors | DK 9A | Bearings | Plain |
| Gear ratio | 68:16 | Brakes | Hand, rheostatic, Maley mechanical track |
| Truck | Brill 21E<br>Hurst Nelson 21E | Controllers | DK DB1 K3 |
| Wheelbase | 6′6″ | Seats | 36.22:58 |

1948 classification A1.

Nos. 294, 312, 330–9 with Hurst Nelson trucks in 1945.

Nos. 294/7/8, 300/10/2 with Maley mechanical track brakes in 1945.

No. 332 with Peckham P.22 truck, 7′6″ wheelbase and from 1926 M&T air track magnetic track, and mechanical track brakes. Enclosed (seats 40.22:62) and fitted with new stairs and platform doors, 1935/6. Classified A3 in 1948 and renumbered 338.

No. 321 rebuilt December 1937 with M&T air track, magnetic track and mechanical track brakes, Peckham P.22 truck, 7′6″ wheelbase 30 B1 motors, enclosed (seats 40.22:62) new platforms, platform doors, new stairs and flush panelled sides. Classified A3 in 1948 and renumbered 337.

No. 339 enclosed (seats 40.22:62) and fitted with new stairs and platform doors March 1942. Classified A2 in 1948. Fitted November 1948 with Peckham P.22 trucks, without air brakes, 7′6″ wheelbase and reclassified A3/RHEO.

A number of balcony cars were fitted with indicator number boxes 1928–30, including Nos. 298, 302/14/23/4/8.

Withdrawn: 313 dismantled for fire watching duties about 1940.
Remaining balconies, 1 in 1944, 39 in 1945, 2 in 1946, 1 in 1947, 1 in 1948.
Nos. 299, 317/8/24/6 sold for use as bungalows.
Enclosed cars 1 (338(332)) in 1949, 1 (337(321)) in 1950, 1 (339) in 1951.

*1919–23 Nos. 340–69*
Hamilton designed, Leeds built double deckers, vestibuled but with open top deck balconies. Identical with 293–339.

| | | | |
|---|---|---|---|
| No. of cars | 30 | Wheel diameter | 32″ |
| Motors | DK 30 B1 | Bearings | Plain |
| Gear ratio | 68:16 | Brakes | Hand, rheostatic |
| Truck | Hurst Nelson 21E<br>Peckham P.22 | Controllers | DK DB1 K3 |
| Wheelbase | 6′6″, 7′6″ | Seats | 36.22:58 |

1948 classification A2, A3, A3/2.

Nos. 346/7/9/50/4–9/61–9 Peckham P.22 trucks, 7′6″ wheelbase.

Nos. 346/7/9/50 equipped from 1926 with M&T Air track, magnetic track and mechanical track brakes – classified A3 in 1948.

Nos. 354–9/61–9 equipped from 1926 with EMB Air track, magnetic track and mechanical track brakes – classified A3/2 in 1948.

Nos. 344/8 equipped with 7′6″ wheelbase Hurst Nelson trucks, classified A2/LWB in 1948.

Nos. 351/60 equipped with DK9A motors – classified A2/DK9A in 1948.

No. 362 had Hoffmann roller bearings for a period.

All, except 342, enclosed (seats 40.22:62) 1935/6 and fitted with new stairs and platform doors.

No. 342 had large route number boxes.

Withdrawn: 1 (342) in 1946, 1 in 1947, 2 in 1948, 23 in 1949, 2 in 1950, 1 (359) in 1951.

*1923–5 Nos. 370–92*
Hamilton designed, Leeds built enclosed double deckers, the first in Leeds, the first five (370–5) having reversed stairs, the remainder standard.

| | | | |
|---|---|---|---|
| No. of cars | 23 | Wheel diameter | 32″ |
| Motors | DK 30 B1 | Bearings | Plain |

| | | | |
|---|---|---|---|
| Gear ratio | 68:16 | Brakes | Hand and rheostatic |
| Truck | Peckham P.22 | Controllers | DK DB1 K3<br>DK DB1 K4 |
| Wheelbase | 7′6″ | Seats | 46.24:70 |

1948 classification A3/2, A3/3.

All equipped with EMB air track, magnetic track and mechanical track brakes from 1926.

All equipped with modified indicators with large number boxes and 'via' blinds from 1926.

Nos. 371/2/4–6 equipped with DK DB1 K3 controllers, classified A3/2 in 1948.

Nos. 370/3/7–92 equipped with DK DB1 K4 controllers, classified A3/3 in 1948.

No. 389 equipped with plain bearing, 7′6″ wheelbase Peckham P.35 truck – no air or mechanical track brakes, classified A3/3/RHEO in 1948.

No. 392 equipped with Craven truck classified A3/3/CRAVEN in 1948.

No. 390 fitted with roof guttering.

Withdrawn: 3 in 1949, 6 in 1950, 12 in 1951, 2 (375/7) in 1952.

*1925–6 Nos. 393–9, 401–5*
Hamilton designed, Leeds built, enclosed double deckers. 393–5 similar to 370–92 but the remainder (built from December 1925) with roof guttering.

| | | | |
|---|---|---|---|
| No. of cars | 12 | Wheel diameter | 32″ |
| Motors | DK 30 B1 :<br>†DK 83 B4 | Bearings | Plain |
| Gear ratio | 68:16 :<br>†61:14 | Brakes | Hand and rheostatic |
| Truck | Peckham P.22 :<br>†EMB Pivotal | Controllers | DK DB1 K4 :<br>†DK DB1 K33E |
| Wheelbase | 7′6″ :<br>†10′0″ | Seats | 46.24:70 |

1948 classification: A3/3, †B3

Nos. 393–8, 402–5 originally with equipment marked † but Nos. 393, 402 later altered to P.22 truck etc.

Nos. 399, 401 originally with 'unmarked' equipment, but 401 later altered to † equipment.

Nos. 394/5 at first equipped with air brakes, soon removed.

No. 396 fitted with Hoffmann roller bearings, but in January 1950 mounted experimentally on EMB 9′0″ wheelbase flexible axle truck (ex-Liverpool), 27″ wheels and MV 116 motors. This exchanged with Horsfield 179 in July 1950 when 396 acquired a Peckham P.35 Skefco roller bearing truck, 8′6″ wheelbase, WT28S motors. Not reclassified.

No. 397 equipped with MV OK 9B controllers, GEC WT 32 motors, gear ratio 70:14, classified B3/WT32/OK9B in 1948.

No. 402 retained DK DB1 K33E controllers with P.22 truck etc. and classified A3/2/K33E in 1948.

No. 404 equipped with MV OK 9B controllers and MV 114 motors (67:14 gears) – classified B3/MV114/OK9B in 1948.

Nos. 393/9, 402 equipped with EMB air track, magnetic track and mechanical track brakes from 1926.

All cars fitted with indicator number boxes and 'via' route blinds from 1926, except 404/5 so built.

Withdrawn: 1 in 1950, 8 in 1951, 2 in 1952, 1 (396) in 1953.

*1925 No. 400*

Chamberlain designed, Leeds built enclosed double decker, the prototype for the 'Chamberlain' cars and the first to have route number indicators. The route number blind was in the usual position in the front top deck windows, but the destination and route blinds were in the front panelling. This disposition was not repeated, but this car was never altered.

| | | | |
|---|---|---|---|
| No. of cars | 1 | Wheel diameter | 32″ |
| Motor | DK 83 B4 | Bearings | Plain |
| Gear ratio | 61:14 | Brakes | hand, rheostatic |
| Trucks | EMB Pivotal | Controllers | DK DB1 K33E |
| Wheelbase | 10′0″ | Seats | 46.26:72 |

1948 classification B3.

Withdrawn: October 1951.

*1926–27 Nos. 76–150*

Chamberlain designed, English Electric built enclosed double deckers.

| | | | |
|---|---|---|---|
| No. of cars | 75 | Wheel diameter | 32″ |
| Motors | MV 114 | Bearings | Plain, Hoffmann Roller |
| Gear ratio | 67:14 | Brakes | Hand, rheostatic |
| Trucks | EMB Pivotal | Controllers | MV OK 9B |
| Wheelbase | 10′0″ | Seats | 46.26:72 |

1948 classification B2.

Nos. 90, 102/7/17/9/29/44/8/50, plus some others, equipped with Hoffmann Roller bearings. No. 117 altered to plain 1952.

No. 85 equipped with WT 32 motors, 70:14 gear ratio, DK DB1 K33E controllers, substituted before 1948 by MV OK 9B – classified B2/WT 32 in 1948.

Nos. 82/7 equipped with platform doors about 1933.

No. 89 equipped with lower saloon transverse seating about 1933 – capacity 46.22:68.

No. 147 equipped in 1944 with Peckham P.35 truck, BTH 509 motors, 58:15 gear ratio, 27″ wheels, 8′6″ wheelbase – classified B2/27/BTH/5815 in 1948. Soon afterwards re-equipped with standard 32″ wheels, MV 114 motors, 67:14 gear ratio.

All except 85/6, 104/17–9/21/7/9/33/44/6/8/50 equipped with Peckham P.35 trucks 8′6″ wheelbase, Skefco roller bearings, 1944–52. Not identified in 1948 classification.

No. 78 ran 1948–51 with Skefco roller bearing Peckham P.22 truck (described as 'Edinburgh') – classified B2/3 in 1948.

Nos. 84/5, 91/9, 100/6/7/9/26/30/4/5/46/8 modified with single blind indicators 1949–53.

Withdrawn: Pivotals 1 in 1942 (fire), 4 in 1953, 9 in 1954.
P.35s 1 in 1951, 1 in 1952, 3 in 1954, 20 in 1955, 36 in 1956.

*1926–27 Nos. 1–10, 49–52, 55–75*

Chamberlain designed Brush built enclosed double deckers.

| | | | |
|---|---|---|---|
| No. of cars | 35 | Wheel diameter | 32″ |
| Motors | MV 114 | Bearings | Plain, Hoffmann Roller |
| Gear ratio | 67;14 | Brakes | Hand and rheostatic |
| Truck | EMB Pivotal | Controllers | MV OK 9B |
| Wheelbase | 10′0″ | Seats | 46.26:72 |

1948 Classification B1

Nos. 5, 66/9, 70/3/5 and some others with Hoffman Roller Bearings, No. 70 altered from Hoffmann to plain.

All except 5, 50/2/8, 61/3/6/9, 70/3/5 equipped with Peckham P.35 8′6″ wheelbase, Skefco roller bearinged trucks 1946–9, not separately identified in 1948 classification.

Nos. 1, 8, 49, 60, 70 modified with single blind indicators 1949–52.

Nos. 24/8/9, 39 altered to this class 1950–2 but not reclassified.
Withdrawn: Pivotals – 3 in 1951, 8 in 1953, 2 in 1954
P.35s – 1 in 1952, 14 in 1955, 12 in 1956
(above figures include cars incorporated from class B1/2 below)

*1926–7 Nos. 11–48, 53, 54*
Chamberlain designed, Brush built enclosed double deckers only electrically different from above batch.

| | | | |
|---|---|---|---|
| No. of cars | 40 | Wheel diameter | 32″ |
| Motors | GEC WT 32R | Bearings | Plain |
| Gear ratio | 70:14 | Brakes | Hand, rheostatic |
| Truck | EMB Pivotal | Controllers | DK DB1 K33 |
| Wheelbase | 10′0″ | Seats | 46.26:72 |

1948 classification B1/2

No. 24 equipped with MV 114 motors and EMB air brakes until 1938. Classified B1/2/MV 114 in 1948. Equipped with Peckham P.35, 8′6″ wheelbase truck, Skefco roller bearings in 1947 and MV OK 9B controllers about 1951, not officially reclassified to B1.

No. 39 equipped with MV 114 motors, and M&T air brakes until 1938. Classified B1/2 in 1948. Equipped with Peckham P.35, 8′6″ wheelbase truck, Skefco roller bearings in 1947 and MV OK 9B controllers about 1951. Not officially reclassified to B1.

No. 44 fitted with lower saloon transverse seating about 1933, seating capacity 46.22:68.

Nos. 15/6 equipped with BTH 510H controllers 1950. Not reclassified.

Nos. 11, 30/1/6, 45/6 equipped with MV OK 9B controllers 1950–1. Not reclassified.

Nos. 28/9 equipped with MV OK 9B controllers, MV 114 motors, 67:14 gearing Hoffmann roller bearings in 1952. Not officially reclassified to B1.

Nos. 16, 45 modified with single blind indicators 1949–50.

Nos. 12, 34/8, 44 equipped with Peckham P.35 trucks, 8′6″ wheelbase Skefco roller bearings, GEC WT 28S motors, 59:16 gear ratio and 27″ wheels 1948–9, classified B1/3.

Nos. 34/8 equipped with MV OK 9B controllers 1950–1, but not reclassified.

Withdrawn: B1/2 – 3 in 1951, 11 in 1952, 14 in 1953, 3 in 1954
B1/3 – 1 in 1954, 3 in 1955.

*1926–27 Nos. 411–445*
Chamberlain designed, Leeds built enclosed double deckers.

| | | | |
|---|---|---|---|
| No. of cars | 35 | Wheel diameter | 32″ |
| Motors | MV 114 | Bearings | Hoffmann roller, plain |
| Gear ratio | 67:14 | Brakes | Hand, rheostatic |
| Trucks | EMB Pivotal | Controllers | MV OK 9B |
| Wheelbase | 10′0″ | Seats | 46.26:72 |

1948 classification B3/2

Nos. 411/2/4/5/8/9/22/7/35/45 with plain bearings after 1944 : possibly others earlier.

Nos. 420/3/39 equipped with Peckham P.35 truck, 8′6″ wheelbase and Skefco roller bearings 1946–9.

Nos. 433/4 equipped 1945 and 1948 respectively with Peckham P.35 truck, 8′6″ wheelbase, Skefco roller bearings, GEC WT 28 motors, 59:16 gear ratio, 27″ wheels, classified B3/3 in 1948.

No. 428 modified with single blind indicators 1950.

Withdrawn: Pivotals – 3 in 1951, 6 in 1952, 20 in 1953, 1 in 1954 (425)
P.35s – 1 in 1953, 1 in 1954, 3 in 1955.

*1928 Nos. 406–10*
Hamilton style, Leeds built enclosed double deckers of modified design with full indicators and 18ft bodies.

| | | | |
|---|---|---|---|
| No. of cars | 5 | Wheel diameter | 32″ |
| Motors | MV 114 | Bearings | Plain |
| Gear ratio | 67:14 | Brakes | Hand, rheostatic |
| Trucks | EMB Pivotal | Controllers | MV OK 9B |
| Wheelbase | 10′0″ | Seats | 46.24:70 |

1948 classification B3/2

No. 406 equipped with DK 83 B4 motors, 61:16 gear ratio, DK DB1 K33E controllers, classified B3 in 1948.

No. 408 equipped in 1949 with Peckham P.35 truck, 8′6″ wheelbase, Skefco roller bearings.

Withdrawn: Pivotals – 3 in 1951, 1 in 1952
P.35 – 1 in 1955

*1930 Nos. 151–4*
Horsfield designed, Leeds built experimental double deck fully enclosed cars, with transverse lower deck seating and flush side panels.

No. of cars – 4 with different equipment.

| | 151 | 153 | 152 | 154 |
|---|---|---|---|---|
| Motors | GEC WT 28 | GEC WT 28 | BTH A12 (later BTH 509) | BTH A12 (later BTH 509) |
| Gear ratio | 59:16 | 59:16 | 58:15 | 58:15 |
| Truck | Smith Pendulum | EMB Flexible axle | Peckham P.35 | Peckham P.35 |
| Wheelbase | 8′6″ | 8′6″ | 8′6″ | 8′6″ |
| Wheel diam. | 27″ | 27″ | 27″ | 27″ |
| Bearings | Plain | Skefco roller | Hoffmann roller | Hoffmann roller |
| Controllers | GEC KA1 | GEC KA1 | BTH 525A | BTH 525A |
| 1948 class'n | C1 | C1/FLEX | C2 | C2/PETERS |

Brakes (except 154) M&T air wheel, air track, magnetic track, mechanical track, hand.

Seats (all cars) 37.23:60

All fitted with platform doors about 1933.

No. 151 equipped with Peckham P.35 Skefco roller bearing truck about 1931, and BTH 525A controllers after 1948 – not reclassified.

No. 154 had Peters air brake equipment until about 1950, not reclassified when this was replaced by M&T. At all times it had air wheel, air track, magnetic track, mechanical track and handbrakes.

Nos. 152/4 finally equipped with Skefco roller bearings.

Nos. 151/2 modified with single blind indicators 1950–2.

Withdrawn: 1 in 1958, 3 in 1959.

*1931 Nos. 155–204*
Horsfield designed, Brush built production series of previous design with BTH electrical equipment.

| | | | |
|---|---|---|---|
| No. of cars | 50 | Wheel diameter | 27″ |
| Motors | BTH A12 then BTH 509 | Bearings | Hoffmann roller |
| Gear ratio | 58:15 | Brakes | M&T Air wheel, air |

| | | | |
|---|---|---|---|
| Truck | Peckham P.35 | | track, magnetic track, mechanical track and hand |
| Wheelbase | 8′6″ | Controllers | BTH 525A |
| | | Seats | 37.23:60 |

1948 classification C2/2

All equipped with platform doors about 1933.

No. 166 modified in 1934 with Crompton Parkinson C151 A6 motors, CT TE1 controllers and air wheel brake equipment, classified C2/2/CP/AW. Re-quipped as standard C1/2 about 1951 and so reclassified.

No. 171 equipped with MV 114 motors, 32″ wheel diameter, 67:14 gear ratio, classified C2/2/MV.114 in 1948. Re-equipped to standard C2/2 April 1951 – so reclassified, but without mechanical track brakes. Skefco roller bearings throughout.

No. 204 equipped in June 1945 with M&T Hornless truck, MV 114 motors, 32″ wheel diameter, 67:14 gear ratio, Skefco roller bearings, classified C2/2/HORNLESS/MV114 in 1948. In October 1951 re-equipped with 27″ wheels, WT28 motors, retaining Skefco roller bearings, classified C2/2/WT28. No mechanical track brakes after 1945.

Nos. 180/4 equipped with BTH 502 motors, not separately classified.

Nos. 168/76/7/9/80/3/4, 200/1 with Skefco roller bearings, but after 1953 all except 162 so fitted at various times, few being withdrawn fitted with Hoffmann bearings.

No. 187 with experimental internal panelling, seating reduced to 33.23:56, later increased to 35.23:58.

Nos. 163/7/75/87/90 equipped with WT28 motors at various times but not more than three at once.

No. 179 equipped in 1951 with EMB flexible axle truck, 9′0″ wheelbase, MV 116 motors, improved air wheel brake. No special reclassification given. In March 1953 restored to class C2/2 (Hoffmann bearings at first.)

Nos. 155/7–65/7/9–72/5/7–9/81/4–95/8/9, 200–2/4 fitted with single blind indicators and pullman ventilators 1950–57,excepts Nos. 161/3/4/88/90/5, 201 with single blind indicators only 1956/7.

Nos. 155/60 with pullman ventilators only 1949–56.

No. 177 had pullman ventilators added after single blind indicator.

Nos. 191, 204 had pullman ventilators in centre windows.

Withdrawn: 1 in 1957, 1 in 1958, 47 in 1959.

*1931–2 Nos. 205–54*
Horsfield designed, Brush built cars, identical with previous batch except for GEC electrical equipment.

| | | | |
|---|---|---|---|
| No. of cars | 50 | Wheel diameter | 27″ |
| Motors | GEC WT 28S | Bearings | Skefco roller |
| Gear ratio | 59:16 | Brakes | Peters air wheel, air |

| | | | |
|---|---|---|---|
| Truck | Peckham P.35 | | track, magnetic track, mechanical track, hand |
| Wheelbase | 8′6″ | Controllers | GEC KA1 |
| 1948 Classification C1/2 | | Seats | 37.23:60 |

Nos. 220/42 equipped with Hoffmann roller bearings at different times, 242 also with BTH 509 motors latterly.

Nos. 214/29/46/52/3 fitted with OK9B controllers 1955, not reclassified.

Nos. 209/13/4/29/52 re-motored 1955 (? MV 101) not reclassified.

Nos. 205/9/10/5/8/20/6/8/31/2/5/7–41/4/6/9/52/4 modified with single blind indicators and pullman ventilators 1950–53.

Nos. 207/21/36 fitted with pullman ventilators only.

No. 166 added to this class about 1951, and fitted with single blind indicators and pullman ventilators 1957, also OK9B controllers 1957 – not reclassified.

Withdrawn: 21 in 1955, 5 in 1956, 4 in 1957, 3 in 1958, 18 in 1959.

*1933 No. 255*

Vane Morland designed, Brush built experimental high speed enclosed double decker, for Middleton route.

| | | | |
|---|---|---|---|
| No. of cars | 1 | Wheel diameter | 27″ |
| Motors | MV 109 | Bearings | Hoffmann roller |
| Gear ratio | 68:13 | Brakes | M&T air wheel, air track, magnetic track and hand |
| Bogies | M&T swing link | Controllers | MV OK 42B |
| Wheelbase | 14′0″ (4′6″) | Seats | 40.30:70 |

1948 classification D1

Originally equipped with two trolley poles.

Modified in 1952 with GEC WT 181A motors, 71:14 gear ratio and MV EP controllers to permit satisfactory operation alongside standard cars. Modified with single blind indicators 1953.

Withdrawn: 1956.

*1935 Nos. 256–271*

Vane Morland designed, Brush built (256–263) or English Electric built (264–271) production series of previous class. Body 6″ shorter than 255 and detail differences, also minor detail differences between Brush and English Electric cars.

| | | | |
|---|---|---|---|
| No. of cars | 16 | Wheel diameter | 27″ |
| Motors | GEC WT 181A | Bearings | Hoffmann roller |
| Gear ratio | 71:14 | Brakes | M&T air wheel, air track, magnetic track, hand |

| | | | |
|---|---|---|---|
| Bogies | M & T Swing Link | Controllers | MVEP |
| Wheelbase | 13′6″ (4′6″) | Seats | 40.30:70 |

1948 classification Brush cars D2, English Electric cars D3.

All modified with single blind indicators 1950–3 and with deeper guttering at the ends 1951–53.

Withdrawn: 12 in 1956, 4 in 1957.

*1935 Nos. 272–274*
Vane Morland designed, Leeds built streamlined four wheeled, enclosed double deckers. Slight body variation between 272 and others.

| | | | |
|---|---|---|---|
| No. of cars | 3 | Wheel diameter | 27″ |
| Motors | BTH 509<br>WT 282S (273) | Bearings | Hoffmann roller |
| Gear ratio | 58:15<br>62:13 (273) | Brakes | M&T air wheel, air track, magnetic track, hand |
| Trucks | M&T swing link | Controllers | DK DB1 K4 (272)<br>BTH 510 (273)<br>GEC KA 10 (274) |
| Wheelbase | 8′6″ | Seats | 26.34:60 |

1948 classification 272:E1, 273:E1/3, 274:E1/2

Built with single blind indicators, but simplified blinds fitted 1950.

Withdrawn: 1 in 1954, 2 in 1955.

*1939–40 Nos. 277–9*
Former London County Council HR2 enclosed double deck bogie cars built non-vestibuled in 1930, but vestibuled before sale to Leeds in 1939.

| | | | |
|---|---|---|---|
| No. of cars | 3 | Wheel diameter | 27″ |
| Motors | MV 109 | Bearings | Hoffmann roller |
| Gear ratio | 68:13 | Brakes | Magnetic track, hand |
| Bogies | EMB Heavy weight | Controllers | OK 29B |
| Wheelbase | 11′0″ (4′9″) | Seats | 48.28:76 |

1948 classification F1

No. 277 equipped in 1943 with M&T air wheel and air track brakes retaining magnetic track brakes, and also with platform doors. Modified with single blind indicators 1951.

No. 278 equipped in 1951 with 'UCC' style air wheel brake, operated by standard Leeds style valve, retaining magnetic track brake, also modified with platform doors and single blind indicators.

No. 279 modified with single blind indicators 1953.

Withdrawn: 1957.

*1942 Nos., 446–477 : 1945 Nos. 478–487*
Former Hull Corporation, enclosed double deck cars, rebuilt from older cars

1920–32 (except for 449, Hull 26, which was a new 'replacement' car), some already altered from original condition, and re-equipped 1932–35 with second hand trucks, controllers and motors.

| | | | |
|---|---|---|---|
| No. of cars | 42 | Wheel diameter | 32″ |
| Motors | DK 30 B1 | Bearings | Plain |
| Gear ratio | 66:18 | Brakes | Magnetic track, hand |
| Truck | Peckham P.22<br>Brill 21E | Controllers | DK DB1 K3B |
| Wheelbase | 7′3″<br>7′6″ | Seats | 40.22:62 |

1948 classification G1 Peckham truck cars, G2 Brill truck cars.

Builders: Milnes 1903, originally uncanopied open top, three window body – Nos. 459/67/70/1/7/80/4.
UEC 1909, originally canopied, unvestibuled top covered, uncovered balcony – No. 485.
Hull Corporation 1909, originally canopied, unvestibuled top covered, uncovered balcony – Nos. 446–8/50–8/60/82.
Brush 1912, originally unvestibuled, balcony top covered – Nos. 461–6/9/72/3/6/8/9/81/6.
Brush 1915, originally vestibuled, balcony top covered – Nos. 474/5/87.
Brush 1915/Top Deck Hull 1923 fan light ventilated, three windows, fully enclosed – No. 468.
Hull Corporation 1925, fully enclosed with fan light ventilated three window top deck, and three window body – No. 483.

Nos. 447–51/5/60/5/9 route number in top front window, destination immediately below.

Nos. 459/62/3/6/75/7 route number in top front panel, destination above driver's front window.

Others – route number in top front window, destination above driver's front window.

Nos. 459/64/5/6/9/70/1/6/80/3/4/5 – Class G2 – others Class G1.

No. 448 with DK DB1 K4B controllers, 1948 classification G1/K4B.

Nos. 462/3/72 with DK DB1 K4 controllers, 1948 classification G1/K4.

No. 464 with 70:14 gear ratio, 1948 classification G2/7014.

No. 473 with 7′0″ wheelbase, DK DB1 K4 controllers 1948 classification G1/7′0″/K4.

Nos. 474/5 P.22 truck, 7′6″ wheelbase. 1948 classification G1/7′6″.

Nos. 486 with three window top deck.

Nos. 446–58/60/82 reduced seating: 36.20:56.

No. 462 reduced seating: 35.22:57.

Nos. 463/85/6 reduced seating: 36.22:58.
Nos. 469/72/3/4/6 reduced seating: 38.22:60.
No. 475 reduced seating: 32.22:54.

Withdrawn: G2 class: 2 in 1946, 4 in 1949, 4 in 1950, 2 in 1951.
G1 class: 11 in 1949, 11 in 1950, 8 in 1951.

*1943 No. 104*
Vane Morland designed, Leeds built enclosed double deck 'Austerity' car, replacement for Chamberlain No. 104 destroyed by fire – officially a reconstruction.

| | | | |
|---|---|---|---|
| No. of cars | 1 | Wheel diameter | 32″ |
| Motors | MV 114 | Bearings | Skefco roller |
| Gear ratio | 67:14 | Brakes | M&T air wheel, air track, magnetic track, hand |
| Truck | Peckham P.35 | Controllers | BTH 510 N |
| Wheelbase | 8′6″ | Seats | 40.22:62 |

1948 classification: J1.

Built with single blind indicators, later adapted to take 1949 standard blind.

Renumbered 275 in September 1948.

Withdrawn: 1957.

*1946 No. 287. 1948–49 Nos. 281–286*
Former Manchester enclosed double deck cars, designed by Pilcher and built there 1930–32.

| | | | |
|---|---|---|---|
| No. of cars | 7 | Wheel diameter | 27″ |
| Motors | MV 105 | Bearings | Plain |
| Gear ratio | 62:13 | Brakes | Hand, rheostatic |
| Truck | Peckham P.35 | Controllers | BTH 510 H |
| Wheelbase | 8′6″ | Seats | 40.22:62 |

1948 classification: H1.

Magnetic track brakes removed before entry to service in Leeds, except 287 initially.

No. 287 renumbered 280 in 1948.

No. 281 equipped with EMB flexible axle truck, MV 116 motors, 61:13 gear ratio, Skefco roller bearings in 1950. Not reclassified.

Nos. 285/6 equipped with Skefco roller bearings, GEC WT 28S motors and 59:16 gear ratio in 1951.

Withdrawn: 2 in 1952, 3 in 1953, 2 in 1954.

*1948 No. 276*
Vane Morland designed, Leeds built post war prototype enclosed double decker.

| | | | |
|---|---|---|---|
| No. of cars | 1 | Wheel diameter | 27″ |
| Motors | GEC WT 28S | Bearings | Skefco roller |
| Gear ratio | 59:16 | Brakes | M&T air wheel, air track, magnetic track, hand |

| | | | |
|---|---|---|---|
| Truck | Peckham P.35 | Controllers | BTH 510 N |
| Wheelbase | 8′6″ | Seats | 40.22:62 |

1948 classification: J1/WT 28S

Modified with single blind indicators 1952.

Withdrawn: 1957.

*1949–50 Nos. 290–300*
Former Southampton enclosed double deck cars designed by Baker and built at Southampton 1929–32. Twenty-six rocker panelled cars of similar design built 1923–30 were purchased but not placed in service.

| | | | |
|---|---|---|---|
| No. of cars | 11 | Wheel diameter | 27″ |
| Motors | MV 101 | Bearings | Hoffmann roller |
| Gear ratio | 61:14 | Brakes | Hand, rheostatic |
| Truck | Peckham P.35 | Controllers | MV OK 9B |
| Wheelbase | 8′6″ | Seats | 44.28:72 |

1948 classification: K1

No. 290 entered service with separate number and destination blinds, the remainder with single blind indicators.

Nos. 296/8/9 and 300 had improved '2 and 1' seating, seating capacity 36.24:60.

No. 290 fitted with '2 and 1' seating, capacity 36.24:60, and single blind indicators 1952.

Nos. 298/9, 300 equipped with Skefco roller bearings.

Withdrawn from service: 6 in 1952, 5 in 1953.

Numbers allocated to 301–8/10–2, but these never overhauled and burnt 1951, 6 more stripped outside Leeds in 1950, and 9 never left Southampton.

*1949, 1950–51 Nos. 501–50*
Former MET Union Construction Company 1930 built enclosed double deck cars, purchased from LTE after one car loaned for trial running with its London number, 2099, before becoming 501 in 1950.

| | | | |
|---|---|---|---|
| No. of cars | 50 | Wheel diameter | 27″ and 22″ |
| Motors | BTH 509 P1 | Bearings | Skefco roller |
| Gear ratio | 67:13 | Brakes | Air wheel, magnetic track, Hand parking |
| Bogies | EMB Maximum Traction (LCC class 4) | Controllers | MV OK 33B |
| Wheelbase | Bogie 4′6″ | Seats | 48.22:70 |

1948 classification: UCC/1

All modified with one piece driver's front window and wipers.

No. 530 ran during 1956 with MV OK 9B controllers.

Withdrawn: 1 in 1953, 18 in 1957, 4 in 1958, 27 in 1959.

*1951–52, 1955–6 Nos. 551–590*
Former LUT Union Construction Company 1930 built enclosed double deck cars, purchased from LTE. A number stored in Leeds before being placed in service and Nos. 571/2/5–8/84 never overhauled.

| | | | |
|---|---|---|---|
| No. of cars | 40 (33 in service) | Wheel diameter | 27″ and 22″ |
| Motors | GEC WT 29 | Bearings | Skefco roller |
| Gear ratio | 67:14 | Brakes | Air wheel, magnetic track, hand parking |
| Bogies | EMB Maximum Traction (LCC class 4) | Controllers | GEC K5B |
| Wheelbase | Bogie 4′6″ | Seats | 48.22:70 |

1948 classification UCC/2.

All fitted with one piece driver's front window and wipers.

All cars in service equipped with MV OK 9B controllers 1955/6.

Withdrawn: Service cars: 3 in 1956, 11 in 1957, 8 in 1958, 11 in 1959.
Non Service cars: 7 in 1956.

*1951 No. 301*
Former LCC Bluebird acquired from LTE. Built in 1932 – modernised version of HR2, with separate cabs, platform doors and air brakes.

| | | | |
|---|---|---|---|
| No. of cars | 1 | Wheel diameter | 27″ |
| Motors | MV 109 Z | Bearings | Hoffmann roller |
| Gear ratio | 68:13 | Brakes | EMB air wheel, magnetic track, Hand |
| Bogies | EMB Heavyweight | | |
| Wheelbase | Bogie 4′9″ | Controllers | MV OK 29 BMV |
| | | Seats | 38.28:66 |

Not classified.
Withdrawn: 1957.

*1953 Nos. 601, 602*
Findlay designed, Roe built, centre entrance single deckers intended for high standing capacity.

No. of cars: 2 with differing equipment.

| Wheel diameter | 601 | 602 |
|---|---|---|
| Motors | MV 109 CZ | Crompton Parkinson |
| Gear ratio | 71:13 | 7:1 |
| Bogies | EMB Resilient | M&T Resilient-Inside Bearing |
| Wheelbase | Bogie 5′0″ | Bogie 6′0″ |
| Wheel diameter | 27″ | 26⅝″ |
| Bearings | Skefco roller | Skefco roller |
| Brakes | Air wheel, magnetic track, hand | Rheostatic, battery operated shaft and magnetic |

| | | |
|---|---|---|
| Controllers | MVEP | VAMBAC |
| Seats | 34 | 34 |

Not classified.

Withdrawn: 2 in 1957.

*1953 No. 600*
Findlay designed, Leeds centre exit rebuild of 1931 Brush end platform single decker, formerly Sunderland No. 85, purchased in 1944, mounted in 1946 on EMB heavyweight bogies and used for clearance tests only. Numbered 288 1947–50.

| | | | |
|---|---|---|---|
| No. of cars | 1 | Wheel diameter | 27″ |
| Motors | WT 84 | Bearings | Hoffmann roller |
| Gear ratio | 71:14 | Brakes | Air wheel, magnetic, track, hand |
| Bogies | EMB Heavyweight (Jo'burg) | Controllers | MVEP |
| Wheelbase | Bogie 4′9″ | Seats | 34 |

Not classified

Withdrawn: 1957.

APPENDIX C

# Chronological list of routes opened and extensions made with horse and steam traction

## Horse

| | |
|---|---|
| 16 Sep 1871 | Headingley (Oak) |
| 1 Apr 1872 | Kirkstall (Star and Garter) |
| 3 Mar 1874 | Hunslet |
| 29 Aug 1874 | Marsh Lane (Shoulder of Mutton) |
| 14 Nov 1874 | Chapeltown (Queens Arms) |
| – – 1875 | Headingley extended to Three Horse Shoes |
| 18 Jul 1878 | Sheepscar–Meanwood Road (Buslingthorpe Lane) |
| 1 Jan 1879 | Wortley (Crown) |
| 5 Apr 1879 | Wortley extended to Star |
| – Sep 1887 | Meanwood extended to Ridge View Terrace |
| 1 May 1890 | York Road extended Marsh Lane to Greyhound |
| 20 May 1897 | York Road extended Greyhound to Victoria Avenue |
| 13 Mar 1898 | Meanwood extended Ridge View Terrace to Stonegate Road |
| 30 Apr 1900 | Stanningley extended Castleton Bridge to Branch Road |
| 28 Jul 1900 | Meadow Lane–Malvern Road, Beeston |
| 25 Aug 1900 | Meadow Lane–Wagon and Horses, Elland Road |
| 8 Sep 1900 | Elland Road extended Wagon and Horses to Football ground |
| 22 Sep 1901 | City Square–Whitehall Road |

## Steam

| | |
|---|---|
| 15 May 1891 | Sheepscar–Oakwood (through running from Dispensary) |
| 24 Apr 1897 | Wortley extended Star to New Inn |
| 30 Mar 1898 | Wortley extended Whingate Junction to Whingate |
| 20 Nov 1898 | Meanwood Road–Hyde Park via Woodhouse Street |
| 29 Jun 1899 | Hyde Park–Victoria Road (service via Woodhouse Street) |
| 29 Jan 1900 | Wellington Street–Castleton Bridge (Armley Bridge) |
| 31 Aug 1901 | Wortley (Crown)–Dixon Lane (Lower Wortley) |
| 10 Jan 1902 | Stanningley extended Branch Road–Bramley |
| 2 Mar 1902 | Stanningley extended Bramley–Stanningley |
| 12 Mar 1902 | York Road–Easy Road |

**Traction changes**

Steam replaces horse

| | |
|---|---|
| 7 Jun 1880 | Wortley |
| – Jun 1883 | Headingley |
| 11 Mar 1892 | Kirkstall |
| 10 Mar 1894 | Chapeltown (workings to Leopold Street only) |
| 25 Mar 1898 | Meanwood |
| 13 Jun 1901 | Castleton Bridge–Branch Road |

Steam replaces electric

| | |
|---|---|
| 1 Aug 1896 | Sheepscar–Oakwood (through running from Briggate) |
| 25 Apr 1898 | Harehills–Stanley Road, route extended to Corn Exchange (no service 31 July 1896 to 25 Apr 1898) |

Horse replaces steam

| | |
|---|---|
| 11 Mar 1892 | Headingley |
| 5 Jan 1900 | Meanwood Road |
| 5 Jan 1900 | Meanwood Road–Hyde Park (via Woodhouse Street) |
| 5 Jan 1900 | Victoria Road |

APPENDIX D

# Chronological list of routes opened and extensions made with electric traction

| | | |
|---|---|---|
| 1891 | 29 Oct | Sheepscar–Oakwood: public service 10 Nov 1891 |
| | 11 Nov | Harehills–Stanley Road |
| 1897 | 2 Aug | Roundhay (Canal Gardens)–City–Kirkstall Abbey |
| 1900 | 3 Jan | Sheepscar–Chapeltown (Wood Lane) |
| | | City Square–Headingley |
| | 2 Jun | Corn Exchange–Harehills via Beckett Street |
| | 6 Jun | Marsh Lane and Kirkgate (inward cars only) |
| | | Woodpecker–Victoria Road |
| | 15 Jun | Lower Briggate–Cross Flatts |
| | 24 Aug | Bridge End–Thwaite Gate |
| 1901 | 18 Mar | Meadow Road Junction–Beeston (including extension Malvern Road–Police Station) |
| | 18 Mar | Sheepscar–Hyde Park via Woodhouse Street |
| | 19 Apr | Woodhouse Street Junction–Meanwood |
| | | Meadow Road Junction–Elland Road |
| | 3 Aug | Cardigan Road via Burley Road |
| | | Victoria Road |
| | 14 Oct | Whitehall Road |
| 1902 | 10 Jan | Wellington Bridge–New Inn/Whingate/Dixon Lane |
| | 12 Mar | York Road–Accommodation Road |
| | 2 Apr | Wellington Road–Stanningley |
| | 19 May | Chapeltown (Wood Lane)–Moortown |
| | 26 Jun | Moortown–Roundhay (Canal Gardens) |
| 1903 | 12 Mar | Wortley (Dixon Lane)–Lower Wortley |
| | 3 Sept | St Paul's Street, Westgate, Great Wilson Street, Bishopsgate Street, Hunslet Lane |
| 1904 | 21 Mar | Elland Road–Churwell |
| | 6 Apr | Harehills Road–Compton Road via Stanley Road |
| | 21 May | Domestic Street |
| | 6 Jul | Victoria Avenue–Killingbeck |
| | 8 Aug | Burley Road–Hyde Park via Belle View Road |

| | | |
|---|---|---|
| 1905 | 14 Apr | Bramley Town End–Town Street |
| | 1 Jun | Hunslet Road–Balm Road |
| | | Thwaite Gate–Rothwell (through working Leeds cars over West Riding tracks) |
| 1906 | 16 May | Kirkstall–Hawksworth Road |
| | 9 Jul | Town Street–Rodley |
| 1908 | 4 Jun | Stanningley–Pudsey |
| | 5 Jun | Accommodation Road–Hunslet Road |
| | 11 Sep | Headingley–West Park |
| 1909 | 26 May | Hawksworth Road–Yeadon |
| | 8 Jun | Through working to Bradford |
| | 1 Jul | Yeadon–Oxford Road |
| 1911 | 5 Jul | Churwell–Morley Fountain Street |
| | 20 Oct | Morley Fountain Street–Tingley |
| 1912 | 1 Jan | Morley Fountain Street–Bruntcliffe |
| 1913 | 18 Apr | West Park–Lawnswood |
| 1915 | 9 Mar | Oxford Road–Guiseley |
| | 30 Apr | Killingbeck–Halton |
| | 14 Aug | Cross Flatts–Dewsbury Road |
| | – – | Sovereign Street |
| 1916 | 20 May | Killingbeck–Killingbeck Cemetery |
| | 5 Dec | Stoney Rock Lane (Compton Road direct) |
| 1924 | 18 Apr | Halton–The Beech Walk |
| | 21 Apr | The Beech Walk–Templenewsam |
| | 23 Sept | Killingbeck Cemetery–Crossgates |
| 1925 | 21 Aug | Low Fields Road |
| | 12 Nov | Dewsbury Road–Middleton Arms |
| 1927 | 26 Nov | Middleton Arms–Lingwell Road |
| 1936 | 11 Sep | York Road–Gipton Estate |
| 1939 | 20 May | Dewsbury Road–Waincliffe Drive |
| 1940 | 22 Jul | Balm Road–Belle Isle Circus |
| 1946 | 2 Feb | Belle Isle Circus–Middleton Road |
| 1949 | 6 Mar | Middleton Road–Ring Road |
| 1949 | 28 Aug | Ring Road–Middleton |

APPENDIX E

# Chronological list of tramway service closures

| | | |
|---|---|---|
| 1918 | 25 Mar | Through running to Bradford discontinued |
| 1922 | 15 Jun | City Square–Whitehall Road |
| 1932 | 31 May | Thwaite Gate–Rothwell–also Wakefield service (West Riding Company) |
| 1934 | 30 Jan | Meanwood Road–Hyde Park–Belle Vue Road (Abbyssinia Road) |
| | 5 Jun | Abbyssinia Road–Park Lane |
| | 16 Oct | Hawksworth Road–Guiseley |
| 1935 | 22 Jan | Churwell–Tingley/Bruntcliffe |
| 1936 | 25 Feb | York Road–Hunslet Road via South Accommodation Road |
| | 7 Nov | Halton High Street |
| 1937 | 1 May | East Parade–Burley Road–Victoria Road Bottom |
| | 14 Dec | Domestic Street |
| 1938 | 8 Jan | Elland Road–Churwell |
| | 17 May | Bramley Town End–Rodley |
| | 3 Dec | Stanningley Bottom–Pudsey |
| 1946 | 24 Aug | Copley Hill–Lower Wortley |
| | | Beckett Street–Harehills Road |
| 1947 | 7 Dec | Hyde Park–Cardigan Road |
| 1949 | 3 Dec | Kirkstall Abbey–Hawksworth Road |
| 1953 | 2 Jan | Half Mile Lane–Stanningley Bottom |
| | 3 Oct | Wellington Road–Half Mile Lane |
| 1954 | 3 Apr | Wellington Street–Kirkstall Abbey (section to works kept for service purposes) |
| | | York Road–Compton Road |
| 1955 | 23 Apr | Gipton Approach |

| | | |
|---|---|---|
| | 25 Jun | North Street–Meanwood |
| | | Meadow Road–Elland Road Football Ground |
| | 19 Nov | Meadow Lane–Beeston, also Vicar Lane |
| 1956 | 3 Mar | City Square–Lawnswood |
| | 21 Jul | Boar Lane–Whingate/New Inn |
| 1957 | 28 Sep | Sheepscar–Moortown Corner |
| | | Hunslet Hall Road–Dewsbury Road |
| 1959 | 28 Mar | Briggate–Moortown via Roundhay |
| | | Swinegate–Middleton–Belle Isle–Balm Road Junction |
| | 18 Apr | Bridge End–Hunslet, outward via Neville Street |
| | 7 Nov | Corn Exchange–Crossgates/Templenewsam |

## Sections having no regular service when closed

| | | |
|---|---|---|
| 1944 | 12 Nov | Reginald Terrace |
| | 19 Nov | Marsh Lane–Kirkgate (former inward line) |
| 1945 | 29 Oct | St Pauls Street–Westgate |
| 1946 | 4 Feb | Stanley Road |
| | 22 Sep | Infirmary Street |
| 1957 | 8 Nov | Bishopsgate Street–Kirkstall Road Works |
| | | Low Fields Road Siding |
| 1959 | 7 Nov | Swinegate–Duncan Street–Corn Exchange |

APPENDIX F

# Route numbers

### 1910

1 Roundhay
2 Moortown
3 Meanwood
4 Hyde Park via Woodhouse Street
5 West Park
6 North Lane via Burley Road
7 Hyde Park via Belle Vue Road
8 Guiseley
9 Pudsey and Rodley
10 New Inn, Whingate, Lower Wortley
11 Whitehall Road
12 Churwell, Beeston, Domestic Street
13 Cross Flatts
14 Hunslet
15 Balm Road
16 York Road
17 South Accommodation Road
18 Harehills Road, Compton Road

### By 1926 exhibited from Dec 1925 by cars with new style indicators

1 Roundhay
2 Moortown
3 Meanwood
4 Hyde Park via Woodhouse Street
5 Lawnswood
6 North Lane via Burley Road
7 Hyde Park via Belle Vue Road
8 Guiseley
9 Pudsey
10 Whingate, New Inn, Lower Wortley
11 Rodley
12 Beeston
13 Domestic Street
14 Bruntcliffe and Tingley Mill
15 Dewsbury Road
16 Middleton
17 Hunslet, Rothwell
18 Wakefield
19 Balm Road
20 Harehills via Beckett Street
21 Compton Road
22 Easy Road and South Accommodation Road
23 Crossgates, Halton
24 Templenewsam

### Used from 7 October 1929

1 Lawnswood
2 Moortown
3 Roundhay
4 Guiseley
5 Beeston
6 Hyde Park via Woodhouse Street
7 Hyde Park via Belle Vue Road
9 Dewsbury Road
10 Compton Road
11 Harehills Road via Beckett Street
12 Middleton
14 Pudsey
15 Rodley
16 Whingate, New Inn
17 Halton, Harehills Lane
18 Crossgates
19 Lower Wortley
20 South Accommodation Road
22 Templenewsam
23 Meanwood
24 Bruntcliffe, Tingley Mill
25 Hunslet
26 Balm Road
27 Cardigan Road via Burley Road
29 Domestic Street
30 Victoria Road via Woodhouse Street

### Subsequent changes (excluding closures)

| | | |
|---|---|---|
| 7 | Became Victoria Road via Burley Road | 6 Jun 1934 |
| 21 | Introduced for Gipton Estate | 11 Sep 1936 |
| 17 | Became Harehills Lane | 8 Nov 1936 |
| 20 | Became Halton | 8 Nov 1936 |
| 27 | Became Cardigan Road via Hyde Park | 1 May 1937 |
| 6 | Became Meanwood | 8 Jan 1938 |
| 8 | Introduced for Elland Road | 8 Jan 1938 |
| 11 | Became Gipton Estate | 8 Sep 1946 |
| 27 | Became Belle Isle, Ring Road | 6 Mar 1949 |
| 15 | Became Whingate | 1 Oct 1950 |

APPENDIX G

# Introduction of reserved track

| | |
|---|---|
| 21 May 1922 | Harehills–Oakwood |
| 29 Jul 1923 | Oakwood–Roundhay |
| 18/21 Apr 1924 | Halton–Templenewsam opened |
| 23 Sept 1924 | Foundry lane–Crossgates opened |
| 10 Nov 1925 | Moor Road–Middleton Arms opened |
| 26 Nov 1927 | Middleton Arms–Lingwell Road opened |
| 25 Mar 1928 | Lupton Avenue– Harehills Lane |
| 18 Jan 1931 | Armley Park–Cockshott Lane |
| 24 Apr 1932 | Harehills Lane–Halton Dial |
| 8 May 1933 | Halton Dial–Killingbeck Hospital Entrance |
| 11 Sep 1936 | York Road–Gipton Estate opened (concrete) |
| 8 Nov 1936 | Selby Road Railway Bridge–Halton |
| 20 Aug 1938 | West Park–Lawnswood |
| – –1939 | Cockshott Lane–Greenhill Mount |
| 22 Jul 1940 | Balm Road–Belle Isle Circus (reservation started beyond Railway Bridge) |
| 24 Feb 1946 | Belle Isle Circus–Middleton Road (concrete) |
| 6 Mar 1949 | Middleton Road–Belle Isle Rind Road (concrete) |
| 28 Aug 1949 | Belle Isle Ring Road–Lingwell Road (concrete) |

APPENDIX H

# Leeds tramways – Corporation Ownership

**General Managers**

| | |
|---|---|
| 1894–1902 | W. Wharam |
| 1902–1925 | J. B. Hamilton C.B.E. |
| 1925–1928 | W. Chamberlain M.Inst.T. |
| 1929–1931 | R. L. Horsfield M.B.E. M.Inst.T. |
| 1931–1949 | W. Vane Morland M.I.Mech.E. M.A.I.E. M.Inst.T. F.R.S.A. |
| 1949–1960 | A. B. Findlay M.I.Mech.E. M.I.P.E. A.M.Inst.T. |
| 1960– | T. Lord E.R.D. C.Eng. A.M.I.Mech.E. M.Inst.T. F.R.S.A. |

**Plate 55** 1904 Brush car No. 60 in its final form with vestibules and first style top cover at Kirkstall Road works about 1912

*(Copyright Leeds City Transport)*

**Plate 56** 1897 Greenwood and Batley car No. 14 in its final state with canopies, vestibules and second style top cover outside Kirkstall Road works after an accident, probably 1914

*(Copyright Leeds City Transport)*

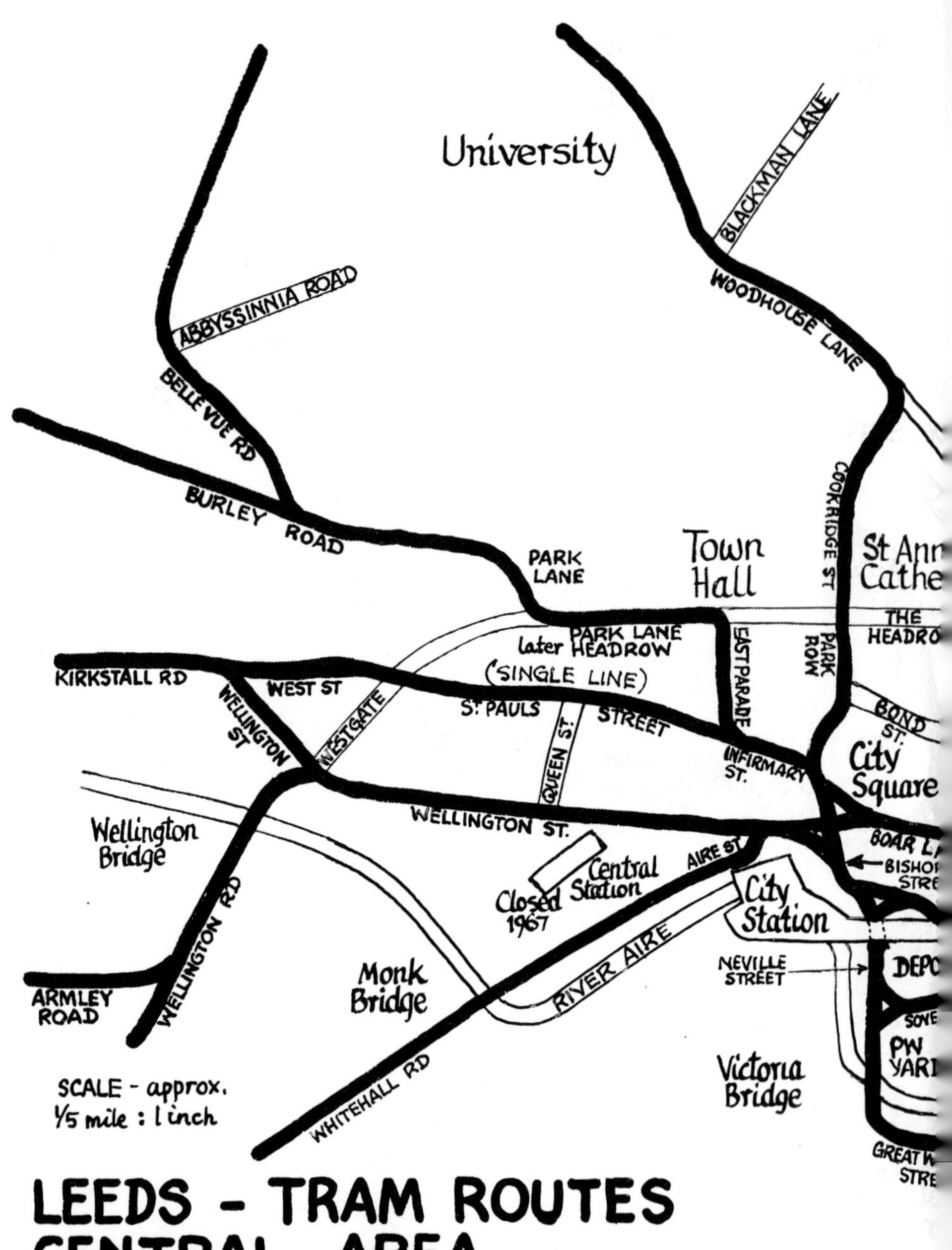


# LEEDS - TRAM ROUTES CENTRAL AREA — ALSO PRINCIPAL STREETS

Based upon the Ordnance Survey 1:10000 map with the permission of the Controller of Her Majesty's Stationery Office

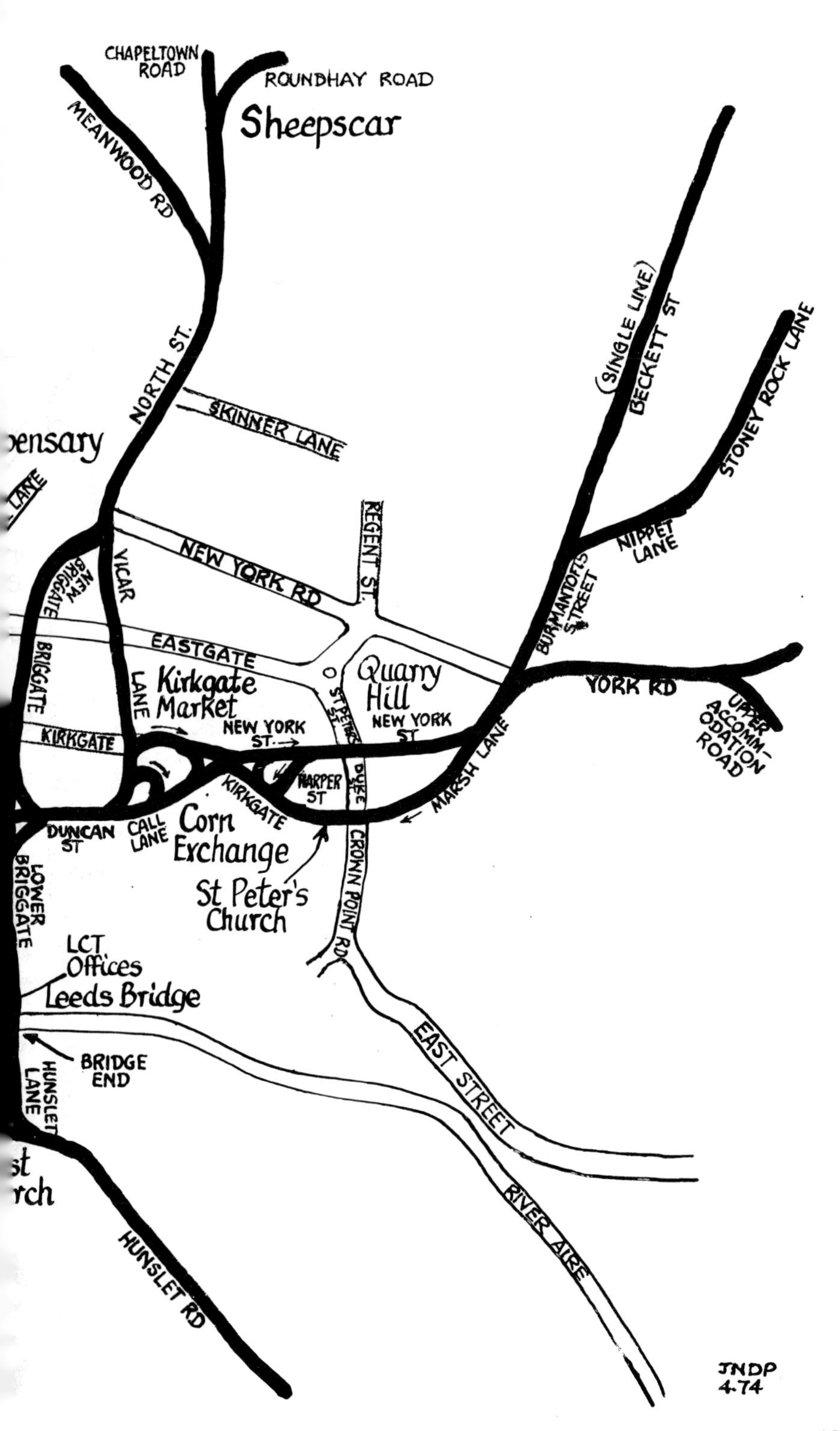
CHAPELTOWN ROAD
ROUNDHAY ROAD
Sheepscar
MEANWOOD RD
NORTH ST.
SKINNER LANE
(SINGLE LINE)
BECKETT ST
STONEY ROCK LANE
NIPPET LANE
REGENT ST.
NEW YORK RD
BURMANTOFTS STREET
NEW BRIGGATE
VICAR
EASTGATE
Quarry Hill
YORK RD
UPPER ACCOMMODATION ROAD
BRIGGATE
LANE
Kirkgate Market
NEW YORK ST.
NEW YORK ST
KIRKGATE
ST PETERS ST
MARSH LANE
HARPER ST
DUKE ST
KIRKGATE
DUNCAN ST
CALL LANE
Corn Exchange
CROWN POINT RD
LOWER BRIGGATE
St Peter's Church
LCT Offices
Leeds Bridge
BRIDGE END
HUNSLET LANE
EAST STREET
RIVER AIRE
HUNSLET RD
JNDP 4.74

# Bibliography


Annual Reports and Statistics, Leeds City Tramways Committee

Buses Illustrated 1965 'Bathing vans, showboats and kipper boxes', F. G. Simons

Buses, Trolleys and Trams, Chas. S. Dunbar

City of Leeds - A short history of civic housing

Development of Suburban Transport in Leeds (Journal of Transport History 4), G. C. Dickinson

Electrician (various issues)

History of the Steam Tram, Dr. H. A. Whitcombe

Leeds City Tramways Guide 1911, Alfred Mattison

Leeds Corporation Acts (various 1871–1946)

Leeds, A Guide and History, Joseph Lee

Modern England, Sir J. A. R. Marriott

Modern Tramway esp. Trams in Leeds, C. H. Crowther, Aug 1969; Bradford to Leeds, J. S. King, Jun 1969; Leeds Trams 1939–59, Andrew D. Young, Jun '72–Feb '74

Modern Tramway Review – Remember Leeds Trams, A. K. Terry

Ministry of Transport Accident Reports, Churwell and Oakwood, H.M.S.O.

One Hundred Years of Leeds Tramways, Andrew D. Young

Trams in Colour Since 1945, J. Joyce

Tramway Twilight, J. Joyce

Tramway and Railway World (various)

The City of Leeds – Report on various systems of tramway haulage, Thos Hewson M.I.C.E. City Engineer

Tramways in West Yorkshire (Locomotion Papers No. 13), H. Brearley

Report of Tramways Sub Committee to Highways Committee 1895

Various collected newspaper cuttings – Leeds Reference Library

Leeds Transport Volume 1, 1830–1902, J. Soper

The Tramways of Dewsbury and Wakefield, W. Pickles